Scaling Law

How Visionary Law Firm Owners Use EOS to Build
Value, Step Back, or Exit

Scaling Law

How Visionary Law Firm Owners Use EOS to
Build Value, Step Back, or Exit

Brooke Lively

Contents

Foreword

Entrepreneurship is one of the most exhilarating and disorienting journeys a person can take. As leaders in the world of growth, we've seen what happens when passionate founders face the reality of scaling.

Vision is only part of the equation. Creating structure, clarity, and harmony as a company grows is the true test of leadership. That's exactly where Brooke Lively's *Scaling Law* enters the stage with insight, honesty, and an unwavering commitment to helping leaders build law firms that thrive.

Brooke has spent years inside the financial and operational heart of growing companies. She knows the numbers, but more importantly, she understands the story behind them. You'll find both in this book. The real-world stories of leaders who have transformed their firms, and the practical steps to make it work for you.

Through her experiences, Brooke has codified what many leaders learn only through costly mistakes: how to build a company that grows with stability, purpose, and confidence.

Scaling Law is more than a guide; it's a companion for leaders determined to grow smarter. We've seen the power of clear frameworks transform teams and organizations, and Brooke's voice in these pages brings that clarity to life.

If you're tired of drowning in the details, sacrificing your life to build a successful practice, and trying to figure it out alone, this is the book for you.

– Mark O'Donnell
Visionary & CEO at EOS Worldwide

– Kelly Knight
President & Integrator at EOS Worldwide

Introduction

About five years ago, my fractional CFO company faced a mystery that kept me up at night.

We specialized in law firms, and our team of data-driven women could turn around almost any financial mess a lawyer threw at us. We'd walk into chaos to find firms with no budgets, no cash flow forecasting, and owners who had no idea whether they were profitable. Six months later, they'd have clear metrics, visibility into their data, and the ability to make strategic decisions based on more than gut instinct.

But here's what was driving us crazy: Some clients would get hockey-stick results, while others barely moved the needle, despite getting the same advice from us.

Being the data nerds we are, we decided to figure out what the hell was going on.

We sorted our clients into three buckets:

- Bucket A: Firms showing no discernible improvement
- Bucket B: Firms making steady progress toward their goals
- Bucket C: The hockey stick firms, explosive growth, up and to the right

What were we doing differently with Bucket C that we weren't doing with Bucket A?

Months of analysis later, we had our answer. And honestly? It wasn't anything we could control.

Because it wasn't us.

We were providing identical solutions, identical advice, and identical tools to all three types of firms. The difference wasn't our expertise or our processes.

The difference was execution.

Now, any CFO worth her salt knows that execution is everything. You can have the most brilliant financial strategy in the world, but if you can't execute it, you've got an expensive piece of paper. No basketball team has ever won a game without taking a shot.

But knowing that execution matters and figuring out how to get lawyers actually to execute are two very different problems.

So we dug deeper: What was enabling Bucket C firms to execute so flippin' well when everyone else was struggling?

That's when we discovered something, and everything shifted.

Except for one firm, every single Bucket C client was running on EOS®, the Entrepreneurial Operating System®. Every. Single. One.

The outlier? A firm run by military veterans where they baked accountability into their DNA since boot camp.

Suddenly, it all made sense. EOS was giving these firms clarity of vision, accountability for traction, and healthy teams that got shit done. While other firms were stuck in endless meetings talking about what they should do, the EOS firms were actually doing it.

None of us at Cathcap were surprised by this discovery. We'd been running on EOS ourselves for years. We'd experienced firsthand how Vision, Traction®, and Healthy transformed not just our results, but our sanity. EOS became our number one outgoing referral because we knew that if we could get our clients on this operating system, there was no limit to what they could achieve.

But then we started getting feedback that made my eye twitch.

"EOS Implementers don't understand law firms."

"They don't know how to adapt the system for legal."

"It's hard to find implementers with law firm experience."

Now, I'm going to be straight with you: that's largely BS. EOS works for businesses of all kinds, from landscaping companies to tech startups. The principles are universal.

But lawyers are specialists, and they like working with people who understand their world. They want someone who gets why you can't just "fire all your B-players" when you're in the middle of a major trial. They need someone who understands that law firm partnerships aren't like other business partnerships. They must have someone who won't suggest marketing tactics that violate ethical rules.

Fair enough.

So when my integrator took over Cathcap and asked what I was going to do next, the answer was obvious: become an EOS Implementer® for law firms.

That's why I wrote this book. To show you exactly how thousands of law firms have used EOS over the past 20 years to build the practices they actually want and are more profitable, less stressful, and designed to serve their bigger purpose, whether that's entrepreneurial success or making a meaningful impact on the world.

Because here's what I learned from all that data: The firms that thrive aren't necessarily the smartest or the most talented. They're the ones that execute. And EOS gives you the system to finally, consistently, execute on all those great ideas you've been talking about for years.

Ready to move from Bucket A to Bucket C? Let's get started.

Part 1: The Problem & Possibility

Chapter One

The Wake-Up Call

E very law firm owner is familiar with this moment.

The phones are ringing, clients are piling in, your reputation is growing, and instead of feeling proud, you feel like you're drowning. What used to energize you now feels like clinging to a runaway train with your fingernails. You work harder, stay later, but the problems multiply faster than you can solve them.

Revenue looks good on paper, but cash flow? That's another story. Your team is either walking out the door or walking through it for the first time, basically an HR revolving door. You spend more time putting out fires than practicing law. And at the end of the day, you collapse into bed, asking yourself: "Why is this so hard?"

If that sounds painfully familiar, welcome to the club nobody wants to join. Almost every visionary firm owner eventually hits this wall. Some push through with caffeine and stubborn determination, only to flame out spectacularly. Others plateau, convincing themselves that "good enough" is actually good enough. And a precious few discover that there's a system designed specifically to help them stop reacting and start leading.

What Law School Didn't Teach You

Law school taught you how to practice law, or at least how to pass the bar exam, which isn't quite the same thing. What it absolutely did not teach you is how to hire people who won't drive you insane, fire people without getting sued, manage anyone beyond yourself, build systems that genuinely work, read a P&L without breaking into a cold sweat, or scale a business past the point where you're the only one who knows where anything is.

And that's the problem. One in five attorneys owns a solo or small firm, and law school has left every single one of you completely unprepared to run a business. It's like teaching someone to perform surgery but skipping the part about sterile technique and wondering why patients keep getting infections.

To prove there's another way, that you don't have to white-knuckle your way through entrepreneurial chaos, let me tell you about Constance Wannamaker.

Constance's Breaking Point

Constance is an immigration attorney who built her practice from the ground up, starting in El Paso, Texas, and eventually expanding across multiple states. By every external measure, she was crushing it: a strong reputation, a growing client base, and an expanding team, the kind of success story that gets featured in bar journal articles.

By the time she realized she needed help, Constance was running a 100-person firm doing roughly $20 million in annual revenue. She had offices in multiple cities, a large sales team, and a call center operation that most law firms would envy. But inside the walls of her practice? It felt like barely controlled chaos.

"We were obviously functioning pretty well, but things were messy," Constance told me, with the kind of understatement that lawyers perfect over years of depositions. "Our production work on the cases was a mess. From the time someone signed up to get all the documentation and paperwork and sent it out the door, it took... nine months to a year. And it's the same process every time."

Think about that for a second. The same paperwork. The same procedure. Every single time. And it was taking nearly a year to complete.

But the timeline wasn't even the worst part. The worst part was the errors. "A lot of mistakes, a lot of errors, careless work, people not seeming to care too much about their job," she explained, "which meant a lot of rework, which meant extra time and money."

Every mistake meant starting over. Every delay meant an angry client. Every angry client meant Constance personally handling the fallout. She'd become the chief fire extinguisher in a firm that seemed designed to spontaneously combust.

"I had execution and accountability issues," she said, cutting straight to the heart of it. "For me, as a visionary, I'm spouting out all this stuff that I wanted everybody to do. The accountability was an issue. We didn't have a good structure to figure out where we are going, what we want to do, and how we get there."

Here's what I've seen happen to every attorney caught in this trap: You hand off work without communicating expectations or showing what success looks like. When the results don't meet your impossibly high standards, you yank the task back and declare, "See, I knew I was better off doing it myself." Congratulations, you just built the world's most exhausting hamster wheel.

The firm had grown to impressive numbers, but Constance couldn't control it anymore. "We had a lot of turnover," she admitted. "Clients were not happy because it was taking forever. It obviously was costing us more money. Just more work for everybody and a lot of frustration for everybody."

But here's the thing about Constance: She's not someone who accepts broken processes. So when she realized her firm was running on chaos instead of systems, she started looking for solutions.

The Hidden Cost of "Managing Chaos"

You didn't learn this in law school, but there's a difference between managing chaos and running a business. Managing chaos feels productive: you're solving problems, making decisions, and putting out fires. But you're not building anything sustainable. You're just staying one step ahead of disaster.

The cost isn't just longer hours or higher stress, though those are certainly part of it. The real cost is opportunity. While operational details bury you, your competitors are building relationships, developing new practice areas, and growing their firms.

You're so busy working *in* your business that you never have time to work *on* your business.

Constance felt this acutely. Despite her firm's impressive revenue numbers, she knew it wasn't operating at its potential. "I realized that I was managing chaos more than I was practicing law," she said.

There's a difference between managing chaos and running a business.

"I was trying to keep up with clients, staff, and cases, but there was no structure to any of it. It felt like I was white-knuckling my way through every day."

Her staff weren't failing; they just lacked clarity. Roles overlapped, responsibilities blurred, and accountability was nonexistent. That left Constance as the bottleneck for everything. Every decision, every question, every fire came straight to her desk.

"The stress was bleeding into my personal life," she admitted. She couldn't be fully present with her son. Even when she went for a run to clear her head, she was mentally cataloguing everything waiting for her back at the office.

The Breaking Point

The attorneys who burn out aren't the ones who don't care enough; they're the ones who care too much to let go. Constance cared deeply about her clients, her team, and her work. But caring isn't a business strategy.

The firm was growing, but not sustainably. Revenue was increasing, but profitability wasn't keeping pace, even though they were still very profitable. With costs rising and chaos increasing, Constance realized something fundamental had to change.

"I knew the business couldn't keep growing if I didn't get control of it," she said. "And honestly, I wasn't sure how much longer I could keep going at that pace."

That's the moment every successful firm owner faces. You've built something that works, but it's consuming your life. You're the central hub through which everything flows, which means you can never step away. Growth becomes a trap instead of a triumph.

The cruel irony? Success makes the problem worse. Every new client, every additional staff member, every expansion adds complexity to a system that was already straining. What got you here won't get you there, but you don't know what "there" looks like or how to get there without everything falling apart.

Why This Story Matters

Constance's story is the story of every law firm owner reading this book. Brilliant attorney, natural rainmaker, visionary leader, who suddenly found herself buried under the weight of her own success.

The difference is that Constance found a way out. She discovered that you don't have to choose between growth and sanity, between profitability and personal life, between building something meaningful and truly enjoying the process.

That solution is EOS, the Entrepreneurial Operating System. And it gave her what every firm owner desperately needs: a way to run the business so the business stops running her.

This book will walk you through that same journey: from chaos to clarity, from reacting to leading, and from drowning in operational details to building a firm that grows with intention and runs with precision.

Whether you are already implementing EOS in your law firm or thinking about starting, we'll look at all the best practices and strategies for using this system to your advantage.

Because here's what Constance learned, and what you're about to learn: You don't have to sacrifice your life to build a thriving practice. You just need the right system.

Chapter Two

The Bold Vision

Constance never imagined she'd be running a business. When she graduated from law school, her dream was simple: represent clients, win cases, and make a difference. She wanted to be a lawyer, not a CEO. Yet two decades later, she was sitting at her desk at midnight, staring at payroll reports and wondering when her job had shifted from drafting petitions and waivers to keeping the lights on.

Sound familiar?

Her story isn't unique. Most lawyers never intend to become business owners. But the minute you hang out your shingle or sign on as an equity partner, congratulations, you're no longer just practicing law. You're running sales, finance, operations, people, and strategy whether you like it or not.

For many attorneys, this realization sneaks up like a process server. One day, you're high-fiving yourself for landing your first client. The next, you're stuck negotiating with copier vendors, trying to explain QuickBooks to your bookkeeper, and fielding résumés from associates who think "team player" means showing up in the office twice a week.

Some lawyers try to ignore this reality, clinging to the fantasy that if they just keep practicing law brilliantly, the business side will somehow sort itself out. Spoiler alert: it doesn't. Others embrace it with the enthusiasm of a first-year associate billing their first 2,400 hours, chasing revenue, scale, and empire-building as if their net worth depended on it.

Here's the thing both camps miss: whether you're running toward business ownership or running from it, you're still running a business. The question isn't whether you're an entrepreneur (you are).

> **Whether you're running toward business ownership or running from it, you're still running a business.**

The real question is: what kind of business are you building?

Business Mindset vs. Practice Mindset

Let's start with an uncomfortable truth: Being a great lawyer doesn't automatically make you a great business owner. You can be the sharpest litigator in the courthouse and still run your firm straight into the ground.

Why? Because there's a fundamental difference between a practice mindset and a business mindset.

The practice mindset says: "I just want to serve my clients, do good work, and make a living." It focuses on the craft of law, cases, clients, and courtroom excellence. Independence and control are the highest values. This mindset is where almost every attorney starts, and it's perfectly valid if you want to concentrate on the law.

The business mindset says: "This firm is an enterprise. It needs consistent revenue, scalable systems, people, and processes that don't rely on me doing everything." It focuses on sustainability, growth, and impact beyond what you can personally produce.

Here's the twist most lawyers miss: You need both mindsets, not just one. A firm with only a practice mindset has heart but no legs; it burns out its owner. A firm with only a business mindset has systems but no passion; it feels corporate and soulless. The sweet spot is integration: doing excellent work for clients while running a business that doesn't slowly kill you in the process.

Mike Smith, whom I'll tell you more about in a minute, discovered this balance when he embraced business structure instead of fighting it. "I have always viewed our practice as a business," he told me. "We're in the business of providing quality legal services to our clients. That's basically how I've always looked at it."

That mindset shift, from "I practice law" to "I run a business that provides legal services," changes everything. Suddenly, systems aren't bureaucratic obstacles; they're tools that help you serve clients better. Delegation isn't losing control; it's multiplying your impact.

Common wisdom says, "You can't scale chaos. You can't just hire more people and hope it works. You need systems, you need accountability, and you need the guts to let go."

Constance had to learn this lesson the hard way. She loved practicing law, but as her firm grew, she became the bottleneck for everything. "I was exhausted, and it felt like I was failing at something I never signed up for," she admitted. The turning point came when she finally said the words most attorneys choke on: *I am a business owner.* That shift unlocked everything that followed.

What a Business-Minded Firm Looks Like

So what does this mindset look like in practice? Let me introduce you to two archetypes that prove your motivation doesn't matter, your methodology does.

The Cause-Based Lawyer: This is the attorney who entered law as a calling, to fight for victims, protect families, or give voice to the vulnerable. They measure success in lives changed and by the justice delivered.

Constance exemplifies this perfectly. "I feel really strongly that we need to create more citizens," she told me about her immigration practice. "People who are residents, often one of the biggest barriers for them to become an actual citizen is that they say, 'I can't learn English, and I have to take the test in English.' So we're going to help with that. You have more protection as a US citizen than as a legal permanent resident. We're changing lives. That's what it's really about."

The Entrepreneurial Lawyer: The attorney who sees opportunity everywhere. Growth, scale, and building something significant drive them. They measure success in revenue, expansion, and market impact. These are the folks who see themselves as businesspeople first, attorneys second.

Mike Smith fits this mold perfectly. The founding partner of Smith Barid, LLC, a thriving estate planning firm in Savannah, Georgia, Mike has been building businesses since 2006, when he and his partner, Richard Barid, decided to focus exclusively on estate planning, elder law, and special needs planning. With over 50 years of combined experience, Mike literally wrote the book on living trusts (*The Ultimate Gift*) and was recognized by the *ABA Journal* as one of America's Techiest Lawyers.

But Mike doesn't stop at practicing law. He's launched a registered investment advisory firm, started a coaching program for other estate planning attorneys, and has taken an equity stake in an AI company developing products for the legal industry. As he told me with characteristic enthusiasm, "I've been doing this for over 30 years, and my level of excitement about my firm has never been higher."

On the surface, these two archetypes look completely different, one driven by mission, the other by margin. But peel back the surface, and their business needs are shockingly similar. Both want:

- Predictable cash flow that doesn't depend on their personal production

- A reliable team that shares its values and executes consistently

- Processes that prevent chaos and ensure quality

- Clients who feel genuinely cared for and get excellent results

- The ability to step away without everything falling apart

Whether you're cause-based or entrepreneurial, you want a firm that amplifies your impact instead of consuming your life. And the path to get there is the same: systems that support your vision rather than fighting against it.

This is the irony Constance discovered. She initially resisted a business structure because she thought it would pull her away from serving clients. But once she embraced it, she had more time, energy, and impact than ever before. The systems freed her up to practice law at a higher level while her team carried the operational load.

Future Pacing: Your Firm in Three Years

Close your eyes and imagine your firm three years from now.

If you're cause-based, picture this: Your calendar is no longer a wall of emergencies. You have a team that shares your passion for justice and handles routine work expertly, freeing you to focus on the cases that matter most. Payroll is predictable, clients trust your process completely, referrals flow consistently, and you're making the impact you dreamed of when you first decided to become a lawyer, without running yourself into the ground.

If you're entrepreneurial, picture this: Your firm runs and grows without you having to grind through every decision. You've hired rainmakers, trained leaders, and built systems that scale. Revenue is strong and predictable, year-over-year growth is steady, and opportunities like expansion, acquisition, or even selling are suddenly real possibilities rather than pipe dreams.

And if you're like most attorneys, you probably want elements of both. A thriving practice that makes a meaningful impact, scales profitably, and, this is the kicker, doesn't depend on you working 70-hour weeks until you collapse.

The question is: How do you get there?

There Is a Better Way

Transformation doesn't happen by accident. Firms don't magically evolve into well-run businesses. They get there because their leaders make intentional choices and use proven systems.

For attorneys, that system is EOS.

Now, before you roll your eyes and think, "Here comes another business consultant trying to sell me corporate BS," let me be clear: EOS isn't some rigid framework that'll turn your scrappy law firm into a soulless widget factory. It's flexible enough to honor bar rules, adaptable enough for different practice models, and practical enough that you can actually implement it without an MBA.

For those of you who are already implementing EOS, I'm not trying to reteach everything. But as we return to some of the basics that you may already be familiar with, you'll discover specific strategies and examples of how your law firm can get the most out of this universal system.

EOS focuses on Six Key Components that every business needs to master.

- **Vision:** Getting everyone aligned on where you're going and why

- **People:** Putting the right people in the right seats with clear expectations

- **Data:** Running on numbers and metrics, not gut feelings and hope

- **Issues:** Solving problems at the root instead of just treating symptoms

- **Process:** Making work consistent, repeatable, and scalable

- **Traction:** The discipline and accountability that enables you to achieve your goals

For Constance, discovering EOS was like being handed a roadmap she didn't know existed. Instead of reinventing the wheel or hoping things would improve, she had a proven framework to balance her passion for serving clients with the reality of running a growing business.

"EOS allows you to be a legit business operation," she told me, "whereas before it was really 'How good is the person who's running it?'"

The results speak for themselves. Remember those nine-month case processing times? They dropped to eight days. The constant firefighting? Replaced by proactive leadership. The stress and chaos? Transformed into predictable growth and sustainable profitability.

But perhaps most importantly, Constance got her life back. She can travel extensively, expand into multiple markets, and even start dating again, all while her firm performs better than ever.

Why Now?

The legal industry is changing faster than most attorneys want to admit, and the changes are no longer subtle. Technology is fundamentally reshaping how clients find and evaluate lawyers. Competition is brutal and getting worse by the day. Clients expect transparency, speed, and measurable value, not just billable hours and legal jargon. Margins are shrinking while the cost of good talent skyrockets. And AI is fundamentally changing the way we practice law and train lawyers.

And here's the biggest disruption: As of 2025, non-attorney law firm ownership is already legal in Arizona, Utah, Washington state, and Washington, D .C. Venture capital and private equity groups are already eyeing legal services. And they aren't willing to wait for more bar associations to get rid of Rule 5.4. PE groups are already implementing workarounds in virtually every state to create effective ownership. It's not a question of if this spreads; it's when.

Attorneys who thrive will be the ones who build firms that can adapt, scale, and compete systematically while maintaining excellent legal work.

For entrepreneurial lawyers, this represents the opportunity of a lifetime. For cause-based lawyers, it's an existential threat. Either way, the attorneys who thrive won't necessarily be the smartest or most talented. They'll be the ones who build firms that can adapt, scale, and compete systematically while maintaining excellent legal work.

Here's what's possible when you make that shift: You stop competing on hours and start competing on results, stop being a one-man show and start building something bigger than yourself, and stop *hoping* things will somehow work out and start *making* them work out.

But here's the truth most attorneys won't admit: The biggest obstacle isn't the market, the clients, or even the competition.

The biggest obstacle is you.

Specifically, it's your resistance to letting go of control and trusting systems to do what you've always done personally. Ready to tackle that head-on? Because until you do, all the vision in the world won't matter.

Chapter Three

Why Letting Go Is the Hardest (and Smartest) Move

You can see the vision now. You've started to imagine what your firm can truly become. But here's the part that stops most attorneys dead in their tracks: letting go of the steering wheel.

Lawyers are trained to be heroes. The job practically demands it. Clients expect you to swoop in, solve impossible problems, and deliver flawless results under crushing deadlines. Law school drilled into you that the ultimate responsibility rests squarely on your shoulders. Combine that training with the type of personality that makes a successful attorney, and you end up with what I call heroic lawyering: the owner as the caped crusader, personally handling every client crisis, every strategic decision, and every operational fire drill.

It feels noble. It feels like excellent lawyering. But here's what I've seen after working with hundreds of law firms: heroic lawyering is a beautifully crafted prison cell, and you're holding the keys while complaining about the accommodations.

The very traits that make you a great lawyer, your obsessive attention to detail, your compulsive need to serve clients perfectly, your inability to let anything slide, can trap you as a business owner faster than you can say "billable hours." Left unchecked, they don't create sustainable growth.

They make a very expensive form of self-employment where you've hired a bunch of people to watch you work yourself to death.

Marc's Story: The Micromanagement Trap

Marc Schneider knows this trap intimately, and he'll be the first to laugh about how ridiculous it got. As the CEO, Managing Partner, and Founder of Schneider Buchel LLP, Marc built his firm from scratch over two decades ago, growing it from a solo practice to a 14-attorney powerhouse specializing in community association law across New York. His firm represents co-ops, condominiums, and homeowners' associations, which, if you've never experienced it, involves navigating the special kind of hell where neighbors sue each other over parking spaces and board meetings turn into episodes of *Jerry Springer*.

Marc is smart, capable, and detail-oriented to a fault. He'd earned his stripes not just as an attorney, but as a board president of his own co-op, dealing with residents knocking on his door at midnight during floods and other emergencies. That experience gave him unique insights into what community associations and their managing agents actually needed. Unfortunately, early on, it also convinced him that he was the only person on earth who could understand the intricacies of whether Mrs. Henderson's emotional support peacock violated the building's pet policy.

The firm was growing, which should have been good news. Instead, Marc was drowning in a tsunami of daily decisions that seemed to require his personal attention. Every contract review, every client strategy session, every staffing decision, hell, every decision about what kind of coffee to stock in the break room, flowed across his desk like he was running mission control for NASA instead of a law firm.

His team constantly came to him for approvals on everything from complex legal arguments to whether they could order printer paper. "I felt like I had to do everything. I had to be in control of everything. And I had to know everything, all the way down to the nitty gritty," he told me. "A couple of my buddies laughed at me, but I ordered the refrigerator for our new space when we moved."

Let that sink in for a moment. Here's a brilliant attorney who serves as co-chair of the New York State Bar Association's Condominiums and Cooperatives Committee, capable of handling the most complex real estate disputes in the state, and he's spending his afternoon researching Energy

Star ratings on kitchen appliances. That's not strategic leadership, that's a $500-an-hour refrigerator consultant.

Marc's breaking point didn't come in a dramatic movie moment. It was more like death by a thousand paper cuts, if the paper cuts were client calls during dinner and emails that bred like rabbits overnight. His calendar looked like a game of Tetris designed by someone with serious psychological issues. When asked about it, Marc sighed and said, "All day long, all day long," constantly pulled in seventeen different directions, and still somehow always behind on everything that mattered.

His phone buzzed during client meetings. His email inbox had more messages than a teenage girl's Instagram. He worried that quality would start to suffer, not because Marc wasn't brilliant, he absolutely is, but because even Superman would burn out if he tried to save every cat from every tree in Metropolis while also handling all the paperwork. His whole life was controlled by the firm.

Marc saw the problem and tried to delegate. He'd hand off tasks to associates or paralegals, carefully explaining what they needed to do and when. But here's where it gets predictable: When the result didn't meet his exacting standards (and let's be honest, nothing ever did), he'd take the work back and spend a tremendous amount of time doing it himself.

The message to his team was crystal clear: "I don't trust you to get this right, so just bring me everything, and I'll handle it." Over time, solving the problems themselves seemed pointless. Why bother? Marc was going to redo it anyway. They learned that their actual job wasn't to think or problem-solve, it was to be highly educated errand runners who brought Marc every decision so he could make it "properly."

"I was wearing a lot of hats personally," Marc explained with the kind of weary resignation you hear from parents of toddlers. "I was the COO. I was the CEO. I was the lawyer. I was the person looking at all of the finances. I was the guy ordering refrigerators."

Marc had created a perfect storm of dependency. His team wasn't incompetent; it was their conditioning. He'd trained them like very expensive golden retrievers: bring Marc the problem, get a treat (approval), repeat. Meanwhile, Marc was slowly losing his mind, convinced this was what "maintaining standards" looked like.

Why Heroic Lawyering Always Fails

Marc's experience illustrates a fundamental truth about law firm growth that most attorneys learn the hard way: heroic lawyering doesn't scale. It hits a brick wall where the owner becomes the limiting factor for everything the firm wants to accomplish. And that brick wall? It's surprisingly low.

The scaling problem is basic math, not advanced calculus. There are only 24 hours in a day, and even if you're superhuman enough to work 16 of them, there are only so many decisions one person can make before their brain turns to mush. When you insist on being involved in everything from contract strategy to toilet paper procurement, you create a bottleneck so tight it makes rush-hour traffic in Atlanta, Chicago, or LA look like the German Autobahn.

Your firm can only grow as large as your personal capacity allows, which means you've essentially built yourself a very expensive job with a lot of employees watching you work. Congratulations, you're now the world's most overpaid micromanager.

But the real problem runs deeper than logistics. Heroic lawyering systematically destroys your team's capability while convincing you that you're maintaining quality. When you consistently take work back because it doesn't meet your impossible standards, you teach your people that you don't trust them with anything important. Over time, they stop developing the judgment and skills they need to operate independently.

Heroic lawyering systematically destroys your team's capability while convincing you that you're maintaining quality.

You end up with a team of order-takers rather than problem-solvers. They're like very expensive assistants who can research case law and draft motions but can't be trusted to decide whether to order medium or dark roast coffee without a committee meeting.

The lawyer personality makes this trap especially vicious. You're perfectionists by training and neurosis; you spot every flaw, every risk, every way something could go wrong, including scenarios that would require a combination of natural disasters and alien invasion to actually occur. That hypervigilance serves you well when you're trying to protect clients from worst-case scenarios. When applied to delegation, it's like using a flamethrower to light a birthday candle.

Nothing ever meets your standards because your professional training teaches you to find fault. You can look at a perfectly competent piece of work and immediately spot the three ways to improve it, the two risks it doesn't address, and the one formatting issue that's going to drive you crazy every time you look at it. "Good enough" isn't in your vocabulary, which is great for legal work and catastrophic for building a scalable business.

Risk aversion compounds the problem like interest on a payday loan. Lawyers are paid to imagine worst-case scenarios and protect against them. They're professional pessimists who get rewarded for thinking about everything that could go wrong. When you apply that mindset to delegation, everything looks too risky. What if they miss something? What if they make a mistake? What if they say the wrong thing to a client? Better to just do it yourself; at least then you know it'll be done right.

And then there's your autonomy drive, which sounds positive until you realize it's code for "I don't want anyone telling me how to do my job." Most successful attorneys are independent thinkers who resist having their decisions constrained by systems or processes. You want the freedom to handle each situation uniquely because every case is different, every client is special, and every problem requires your personal touch.

Ironically, this resistance to structure creates a prison where you have to handle everything personally because you've never built the systems that would allow others to handle things competently. You reject the very thing that would set you free because you're convinced it would constrain you.

The hidden costs compound faster than law school debt. Personally, you burn out. Your family starts to wonder if you still live at the house or if they should just forward your mail to the office. Your health deteriorates because stress, caffeine, and takeout aren't actually food groups, despite what your current diet suggests.

Your talented team members leave because they're not challenged or empowered; they came to practice law, not to be highly educated assistants who ask permission to breathe. Those who stay often disengage, becoming professional zombies who wait for direction rather than taking initiative. They show up, collect their paychecks, and save their actual thinking for their side hustles or their next job.

And your business stagnates because growth requires more than one person can provide, no matter how brilliant, dedicated, or caffeinated they are. You've created a firm that can't function without you, which means you can never leave, never truly rest, and never grow beyond what you personally can handle.

Here's the brutal truth: heroic lawyering isn't heroic; it's a trap that limits your firm to your personal capacity while slowly burning you out in a very expensive and public way.

The Better Way: An Introduction to EOS

There's a better way, and it has nothing to do with working harder, hiring more people, or drinking stronger coffee. It's a proven system for running businesses, designed for people who are tired of being the most expensive cog in their own machine.

Thousands of companies across every industry imaginable successfully use EOS. It wasn't designed specifically for law firms, but it works perfectly for them because it addresses the fundamental challenge every growing business faces: how to scale beyond the owner's personal involvement while maintaining quality and culture. In other words, how to build a business instead of an expensive hobby that employs other people.

EOS is a set of simple, practical tools that help you run your business with more discipline and less chaos.

EOS is a set of simple, practical tools that help you run your business with more discipline and less chaos. Think of it as the operating system that runs beneath everything else your firm does. It's the invisible foundation that makes everything else work better, like the difference between a house built by professionals with blueprints and permits, versus the shed your brother-in-law threw together with leftover lumber and a YouTube video he watched once.

EOS gives you a framework for making decisions, solving problems, managing people, and tracking progress without requiring an MBA or fluency in corporate speak. It's designed for entrepreneurs who want to build something bigger than themselves without losing their sanity or soul in the process.

The system works especially well for lawyers because it provides the structure you crave without constraining the autonomy you value. Lawyers love rules and procedures when they make sense (that's why you became a lawyer), but they hate bureaucracy that exists for its own sake.

EOS creates accountability systems that lawyers respect because it focuses on clear metrics and logical processes rather than corporate feel-good nonsense.

Most importantly, EOS builds on your analytical strengths. Lawyers are naturally good at systems thinking once they see how the pieces fit together. Your training guides you in breaking complex problems into manageable components, identifying cause-and-effect relationships, and building logical decision-making frameworks. EOS just gives us a business framework that works the same way your legal mind does.

The beautiful thing about EOS is that it doesn't try to change who you are as a lawyer. It doesn't require you to become some touchy-feely team leader who talks about "synergy" and "paradigm shifts." It gives you the business tools to leverage who you already are more effectively.

Instead of your perfectionism becoming a barrier to delegation, EOS helps you channel it into building systems that ensure quality without your personal involvement. Instead of your risk awareness paralyzing decision-making, EOS provides a framework for systematically managing risk. Instead of your independence making you resist structure, EOS creates structure that increases your freedom by getting you out of the day-to-day operations.

The philosophy is elegantly simple: The owner should work on the business, not in it. Your highest value isn't in reviewing every contract or approving every decision; it's in setting direction, building culture, developing people, and focusing on the work that only you can do. The stuff that requires your $500-an-hour brain, not $15-an-hour administrative skills.

When EOS is working correctly, magic happens, and by magic, I mean logical, predictable results that feel magical because you're used to chaos. The owner focuses on the highest-value work that truly requires their expertise: complex legal strategy, key client relationships, business development, and long-term planning. You know, the stuff you went to law school to do.

The team operates independently with clear guidance about what they should do and how they should do it. They stop bringing you every decision because they actually know how to make decisions within defined parameters. Quality is ensured through documented processes and systematic checkpoints rather than owner oversight, so things get done right without you having to inspect everything personally.

And the firm scales beyond the owner's personal capacity because there are people who make decisions and get the work done without everything flowing through a single, incredibly expensive, and increasingly frustrated bottleneck.

Old Way vs. New Way Comparison

The contrast between heroic lawyering and systematic excellence is like comparing a one-man band to a symphony orchestra. Both can make music, but only one sounds professional and can handle complex compositions without the conductor having a nervous breakdown.

In the old way, heroic lawyering, the owner makes all meaningful decisions, either directly or through constant consultation, leaving everyone feeling like they're bothering their parent for permission to use the bathroom. The team depends on the owner for direction on everything from case strategy to office policies to whether it's okay to take lunch at 12:30 instead of 12:00.

Quality is controlled through personal oversight, meaning the owner reviews everything important to ensure it meets their impossibly high standards. The owner's availability limits growth because everything important requires their involvement, like a business version of helicopter parenting. The owner works in the business constantly, handling operational details and putting out fires rather than working on the business, focusing on strategy and development.

The result? A firm that can't function without the owner, an owner who can't take a vacation without everything falling apart, and a team that feels like they're working for the world's most expensive babysitter.

In the new way, EOS defines systematic excellence, clear roles, and accountability for everyone, so people actually know what they're responsible for and how their performance will be measured. A revolutionary concept, I know. The team is empowered with structured guidance, meaning they can make decisions independently within clear parameters rather than forming a line outside the owner's office every time they need to sneeze.

Documented processes and systematic checkpoints ensure consistency without requiring the owner to personally inspect every paper clip control quality. Systems and a leadership team that can handle increased complexity without the owner becoming a bottleneck enable growth. The owner strategically manages the business, focusing on vision, key relationships, important cases, being the face of the firm, and long-term planning rather than daily operational details that someone earning a third of their salary could handle.

Marc experienced this transformation firsthand, and the difference was like going from performing surgery by candlelight to having a fully equipped operating room. Before EOS, every decision flowed through him, from major client strategy to ordering office furniture. His team brought him every problem, every question, every choice that needed to be made, treating him like a very expensive Magic 8-Ball.

He was working as fast as he could, but he felt like he was always behind, always reacting, always putting out fires that shouldn't have been his problem in the first place. It was like being the emergency room doctor for every minor scrape and bruise in the entire hospital.

After implementing EOS, his team learned to make decisions within clear parameters defined by the firm's core values, vision, and documented processes. They understood what the firm stood for and where they were going, and used that understanding to guide choices about everything from hiring to client service. Systems ensured quality without Marc's personal involvement, and documented processes for client intake, case management, and service delivery meant that things got done correctly and consistently, regardless of who handled them.

Marc could finally focus on what he did best: complex legal strategy, key client relationships, and building the firm's reputation in the community association space. You know, the stuff that required a law degree and two decades of experience, rather than the ability to comparison-shop kitchen appliances. And most importantly, those are the things Marc enjoys doing.

The transformation was so complete that when Marc implemented The People Analyzer®, one of EOS's tools for evaluating whether people fit the firm's culture, two team members who didn't align with the firm's core values essentially fired themselves. "Once we started to put the systems in place with the accountabilities and introduced the core values, they were out," Marc told me. "And let me tell you, it was the best thing that happened."

No dramatic confrontations, no awkward performance improvement plans, no lawyers getting involved. (Not even Marc; his Integrator took care of it!) The system created clarity, allowing people to make their own choices about whether they belonged. It's like natural selection, but for workplace culture.

What EOS Looks Like in Practice

A week in an EOS-run firm looks fundamentally different from the beautiful chaos of heroic lawyering. It's the difference between a well-run restaurant where everyone knows their role and a food truck where the owner is simultaneously taking orders, cooking, serving, and handling the cash register while slowly losing their mind.

Monday starts with the leadership team running a weekly Level 10 Meeting®, a structured 90-minute session in which they review the firm's Scorecard, discuss priorities for the week, and address issues systematically. This meeting isn't the rambling, agenda-free time-waster that passes for meetings in most firms. It's a disciplined conversation focused on keeping the firm on track, with actual outcomes and decisions rather than just updates on how busy everyone is.

Each day, team members check their department Scorecards to see how they are performing against their key metrics. Everyone knows their priorities because they're clearly defined and consistently communicated, not buried in an email from three weeks ago that everyone has already forgotten. Instead of guessing what matters most or trying to read the owner's mind, people can see exactly where they should focus their energy.

Quarterly, the entire firm reviews progress against longer-term goals and sets new quarterly priorities called Rocks. These aren't vague aspirations like "improve client service" or "be more efficient." They're specific, measurable objectives that systematically drive the firm forward, with clear deadlines and defined success criteria.

Throughout, issues get solved rather than managed. When problems arise, and they always do, they go through a structured process designed to identify root causes and implement permanent solutions rather than quick fixes that guarantee the same problem will resurface next month, like a bad rash.

For Marc, this transformation was like going from playing Whac-A-Mole with an endless stream of crises to preventing the moles from popping up in the first place. His team learned to make decisions within clear parameters, following processes that ensured quality without requiring his constant supervision. The best part was that not only did the team benefit from these systems, but the clients did as well.

Client intake followed a proven process that ensured nothing fell through the cracks. Case management followed established protocols, ensuring consistency regardless of which attorney handled the matter. Service delivery met consistent standards because the standards were documented, trained, and measured, rather than existing solely in Marc's head.

Most importantly, Marc could focus on what he did best: building client relationships, developing legal strategy for complex cases, and positioning the firm as the go-to resource for community association law in the state of New York. His expertise wasn't being wasted on operational minutiae or routine decisions that others could handle just as well, or in many cases, better.

The key difference is this: instead of the owner being indispensable, the system becomes indispensable. The firm's capabilities are embedded in its processes, culture, and people rather than residing solely in the owner's increasingly overwhelmed brain. It's the difference between being a one-man band and conducting an orchestra where everyone knows their part and plays it well.

Looking Ahead

At this point, the pieces are starting to fall into place. You understand there's a better way. You can imagine what your firm would look like if you weren't the bottleneck on every decision, if your team operated independently with confidence, and if systems, rather than your personal oversight, maintained quality. You're starting to picture what it would feel like to take a real vacation without your phone buzzing every five minutes with "urgent" questions about office supplies.

But I also know what you're thinking, because I've had this conversation with hundreds of attorneys who were in exactly your position: "Sure, EOS works for other people. Marc made it work. But could it really work for me? Can I actually let go enough for this to happen? What if my team screws everything up? What if clients notice the difference? What if the quality suffers?"

That's the real question, isn't it? The biggest obstacle isn't learning and implementing EOS; thousands of firms have proven it works across every practice area imaginable. The biggest obstacle isn't

The biggest obstacle is the voice in your head.

whether your team can handle more responsibility. Most teams rise to the occasion when given clear expectations and real authority, like flowers that were just waiting for someone to water them.

The biggest obstacle is the voice in your head. The one that whispers, "No one else can meet your standards." The one that insists, "If you want it done right, you have to do it yourself." The one that says, "Your firm is different.

Your clients are more demanding. Your work is too complex for systems."

That voice isn't trying to help you; it's trying to keep you trapped in a prison of your own making, convincing you that the bars are there for your protection when they're really there to keep you from flying.

In the next chapter, we'll tackle that voice directly. We'll address the beliefs that keep you chained to your desk, the fears that make delegation feel dangerous, and the perfectionist mindset that's slowly strangling your firm's growth. Because until you deal with what's really holding you back, all the systems in the world won't set you free.

Chapter Four

Why You Can't Let Go And How to Start

You see the possibilities. You can picture your firm running like a well-oiled machine instead of a circus act held together with caffeine and sheer force of will. But the internal voice saying, "If I want it done right, I have to do it myself," usually stops most attorneys dead in their tracks.

Sound familiar? Of course it does. That voice has been whispering in your ear since your first day of law school, growing louder with every delegation disaster, every disappointed client, every time someone on your team proved that they couldn't read your mind about how things should be done.

The core belief that sabotages every law firm owner goes something like this: "I am the only person capable of doing this work to the standard my clients deserve." It feels logical. It feels responsible. Hell, it feels downright heroic, like you're single-handedly protecting your clients from the incompetence of everyone else in your firm.

After working with hundreds of law firms, I discovered that belief isn't protecting your clients. It's strangling your business and slowly killing your soul in the process.

The problem isn't your team. The problem isn't that you have impossibly high standards (though you probably do). The problem is that you've been trying to delegate without systems, like handing someone a recipe written in invisible ink and then getting angry when they can't cook the dish properly.

Other internal barriers join the party, making things worse. Perfectionism whispers, "No one can meet my standards. Have you seen the garbage they produce when I'm not watching?" Risk aversion warns, "What if they mess up with a client, and I get sued, disbarred, or publicly humiliated?" Control needs insist, "If I'm not directly involved in every decision, I lose oversight, and everything will descend into chaos."

On the surface, these fears sound like diligence. Underneath, they're the bars of a very expensive prison you've built for yourself, complete with a 24/7 guard duty schedule that you can never escape.

Breaking the "I Must Do Everything" Belief

You read about Marc Schneider and his refrigerator-shopping adventures. But let me show you how this prison of "I must do everything" plays out in real time.

I was doing a quarterly session with Moumita Rahman, an immigration attorney who runs a $15 million practice in New York City. One of the issues we were working through was her constant lack of time. Here's the thing about "lack of time": it's never the real problem. It's always the symptom of a deeper issue.

As we started peeling back the layers, we discovered what was really happening. Moumita had boosted a TikTok ad and told her marketing manager to "make sure boosts don't expire." Simple request, right?

Here's where it gets interesting. The marketing manager had a system: Whenever her team initiated a boost, they logged it on a spreadsheet with expiration dates so they never missed one. Solid process. The problem was that Moumita didn't know this system existed, so she had no reason to tell the marketing manager that she'd initiated the boost outside their usual workflow.

Meanwhile, the marketing manager heard "Make sure boosts don't expire," and thought, "Got it covered, we have a system for that." She was thinking about **In the real world "good enough" is often good enough.** what her team did, not what the boss might be doing independently.

Moumita's boost expired.

When Moumita discovered this, something fundamental broke. It wasn't just about a failed marketing campaign; it was about trust. Her internal voice said exactly what yours would: "I can't rely on my team to handle even simple tasks. If I want something done right, I have to do it myself."

The marketing manager, meanwhile, felt the sting of her boss's disappointment and started second-guessing herself. The next time Moumita gave her direction, she followed up constantly, asking for clarification and confirmation. This drove Moumita crazy. "Why can't she just handle things independently like I asked?"

This vicious cycle traps smart lawyers. You delegate something, it doesn't go as expected, so you lose trust in your team's ability to execute. They sense your lack of confidence and become more dependent rather than more independent. So, you take more control to "ensure quality," which confirms to your team that you don't trust them. They stop thinking critically and start asking for constant direction.

Trust, once broken, becomes nearly impossible to rebuild through willpower alone. You can't just decide to trust someone more after they've disappointed you. Your team can't just decide to be more confident after they've felt your frustration.

The marketing manager never followed up to confirm that the team handled the boosts because there wasn't a process for communicating completion. Trust broke down because there was no system to prevent the breakdown. Moumita dove deeper into marketing tasks, leaving her with even less time for the work only she could do.

What went wrong? (Hint: It wasn't the people involved.)

Why Smart Lawyers Get Trapped

You probably don't realize this, but law school trained you to be the exact opposite of a good delegator. From day one, your training teaches you that responsibility for every detail, every comma, every citation rests squarely on your shoulders. Miss a deadline? That's on you. Misquote a case? Career killer. File a motion with a typo? You might as well tattoo "incompetent" on your forehead.

The Socratic method doesn't help. Remember sitting in Constitutional Law, praying the professor wouldn't call on you because you hadn't quite finished the reading? The message was crystal clear: You better know the answer, you better know it perfectly, and you better know it right now. There was no room for "I'll delegate this research to someone else," or "Let me get back to you on that." Complete mastery of every detail, every nuance, every possible angle was expected of you. Otherwise, you might end up the subject of an infamous story like the law student at Baylor who hadn't briefed the case for Evidence, got called on, and the professor ultimately yelled, "I will piss on you like a mongrel dog!" Yes, it's true. And yes, it was my brother. And yes, this is the same professor who grilled the girl next to my brother so hard she fainted.

After years of schooling and conditioning came the bar exam, the ultimate test of individual performance under pressure. No collaboration allowed. No asking for help. No delegating the questions you weren't sure about. Just you, alone in a room, with hundreds of other people proving you could handle anything the legal profession might throw at you. Pass or fail based entirely on your personal preparation and performance.

Now layer on the perfectionist standards that most successful attorneys develop, and it gets worse. Anything less than flawless doesn't feel like practicing law; it feels more like malpractice-ing. What you went through to get to this point in your career is no joke.

Here's something law schools left out of their curriculum: In the real world, "good enough" is often good enough, and perfectionism becomes the enemy of progress. But try telling that to a lawyer who spent three years having every word of every brief dissected and criticized by professors who seemed to take sadistic pleasure in finding flaws.

Combine that with the naturally skeptical nature of most attorneys, questioning everyone's work, poking holes in every argument, assuming the worst-case scenario in every situation, and you've got a recipe for control freak behavior that would make a helicopter parent look relaxed.

One of my clients, a brilliant litigator, perfectly captured this mindset: "I review every email that goes out with my name on it because what if there's a typo? What if they misstate the law? What if they say something that could be taken the wrong way by opposing counsel?" She was spending two hours a day editing emails that could have been sent perfectly well without her input.

Past delegation failures reinforce the pattern like scar tissue, making you flinch every time someone suggests surgery. You delegated without clear systems, the results disappointed you, so you concluded that you're better off doing it yourself. It's a logical conclusion based on flawed data, like deciding you can't cook because your first attempt at baking bread failed because you forgot to add yeast.

This belief doesn't just limit your growth; it's stealing your life. Every task you do that someone else could handle is time stolen from your firm: strategy, new client development, and the work that only you can do. It is also stealing from your personal life: time coaching your children's sports teams, date night with your significant other, or, frankly, just a relaxing Saturday afternoon nap. Every routine decision you make personally is an opportunity missed to develop your team's judgment and capabilities.

There's a way to break free from the "I must do everything" trap. In EOS, we call it the Delegate and Elevate exercise. A simple observation inspires it: surgeons don't empty bedpans. Not because they're too good for it, but because a surgeon emptying bedpans is a $500-an-hour waste of resources that prevents them from doing the work they love, only they can do. Or what Gay Hendricks dubbed the Zone of Genius in his groundbreaking and influential book, *The Big Leap*.[1] Yet lawyers empty metaphorical bedpans all day long and wonder why they aren't happy and can't find time for strategy.

The Delegate and Elevate exercise[2] is a simple clarity tool that forces leaders to get brutally honest about how they spend their time. You list everything on your plate, sort each task into one of four categories: love and great at, like and good at, don't like but good at, don't like and not good at, and then use that visibility to decide what to keep, delegate, or redesign (see diagram on page 38). When leaders spend more time in their Unique Ability®[3] (a concept and term created by Dan Sullivan and explained in his book, *Unique Ability 2.0, Discovery*) and less in low-value or energy-draining work, the organization scales faster, decision quality improves, and bottlenecks shrink. In EOS terms, it's about getting the right people doing the right work at the right altitude.

One of my clients, a successful attorney who billed 2,000+ hours a year and constantly felt behind, decided to map out her activities using this framework. The results were shocking. She was spending most of her time

---

1. Gay Hendricks, *The Big Leap: Conquer Your Hidden Fear and Take Life to the next Level* (New York, NY: HarperOne, 2010).

2. To access the full exercise walkthrough, visit http://eosworldwide.com/Delegate-and-Eleva te-Tool-Download .

3. Unique Ability is a registered trademark, protected by copyright and an integral concept of The Strategic Coach® Inc. All rights reserved. Used with written permission. www.strategic coach.com

on work she either didn't enjoy or wasn't particularly good at, while the work she loved and excelled at got squeezed into evenings and weekends.

"I realized I was the most expensive secretary in the firm," she told me. "I was doing work that someone making a third of my salary could have handled better than me because they wouldn't have been as distracted by all the other things on my mind."

If you do the work to identify what you should delegate, you'll probably discover that you're spending 50–70 percent of your time doing work you don't enjoy and/or aren't particularly good at. A lot of the time, I refer to work that you don't like but are good at as the Martyr Zone or Personal Hell. You do it, but you aren't happy about it. And that category of things that you don't like and aren't good at doing? I like to call that the Suck Bucket. Meanwhile, the work that energizes you and leverages your unique talents, what Gay Hendricks calls the Zone of Genius, only gets 10-20 percent of your time. The immediate insights from this hit like a cold shower. You're not just working on the wrong things; you're systematically avoiding the work that would create the most value.

What Is The Takeaway?

You have to be intentional about the way you spend your time; it is your most finite resource. And the things you are doing should energize you, not drain you. If you did this exercise today (which I heartily recommend), what tasks would you say you "Don't Like"? If you aren't good at it, eliminate or delegate it immediately. These are the tasks that drain your energy and produce mediocre results. For most attorneys, this includes tasks such as updating software, scheduling routine appointments, basic data entry, and managing office supplies.

The things you don't like but are good at are harder to get off your desk. However, they can often be done, with some training, by somebody who will probably enjoy them more than you. Think document review, routine correspondence, or administrative oversight. Just because you don't like doing it doesn't mean somebody else won't love it.

Let's do some math that'll make you wince. If you're billing $400 an hour and spending twelve hours a week on tasks that you don't like that a $25-an-hour assistant could handle, you're burning through $4,800 in opportunity cost every week. That's nearly $250,000 a year in misallocated resources, enough to hire two excellent support staff members and still come out ahead.

But the real cost isn't financial; it's the opportunity cost of the work that isn't getting done. Every hour you spend doing work you don't like is an hour not spent on the work that only you can do: developing key client relationships, creating innovative legal strategies, or building the systems that will scale your firm.

Almost more important than that is the cost to you. When you work on things you like, you renew your energy, you are more optimistic, more likely to find solutions rather than insurmountable problems, and you are just plain happier. You win, your team wins (yes, they like you to be happy, it makes the office more fun), and your family definitely wins!

Your First Delegation Win

Now that you can see exactly where you are wasting your time, let's get you a quick win to prove that delegation doesn't have to end in disaster.

Pick one task from your "someone else could do this" list. Start small, choose something low-risk and routine. It could be updating your case management system, preparing first drafts of standard documents, or handling initial client intake paperwork. Don't try to delegate the most complex case in your pipeline on day one.

Here's the key to successful delegation that most lawyers miss: Systems first. Don't just dump tasks on people and hope for the best. That's abdication, not delegation. Document clearly what needs to be done, step by step. Set expectations by defining exactly what "right" looks like. Create a check-in rhythm so you can catch problems early rather than discovering disasters after they've already happened.

The part that rebuilds trust is closing the loop. When someone completes a delegated task, have that person report back on what they accomplished, any issues they encountered, and what they learned. This simple step transforms delegation from "I hope this gets done" into "I know this got done and how it went." Your team member feels heard and valued. You get confidence that the work is completed properly. Trust grows on both sides.

The magic happens when you give people clear systems and expectations. Marc Schneider discovered this when he stopped assuming his team could read his mind and started documenting his processes. "It took about six months for me to truly delegate decision-making," he told me. "But you've got to really work at keeping people accountable to the fact that if they come to you with something that's not your job anymore, say, 'Hey, I know you want my input, and I appreciate that, but under the new system we have, here's who you go to.'"

What you'll discover is that your team often exceeds your standards when they have clear guidance about what success looks like. They're not failing because they're incompetent; they're failing because they're trying to hit a target you've never clearly defined.

Effective delegation builds trust rather than erodes it. When you delegate with clear systems and follow-through, your team learns they can count on you for guidance, support, and the tools they need for success. You realize you can count on them for results. Each successful delegation creates a foundation for the next, more complex one. Instead of the vicious cycle of broken trust we saw with Moumita's marketing campaign, you make a virtuous cycle where confidence builds with every completed task.

The first delegation win does more than just free up your time. It starts to retrain your brain about what's possible. You realize that the world doesn't end when someone else handles a task you used to do. Quality doesn't suffer just because you're not personally involved in every detail. In fact, it often improves because the person you delegated to can focus on doing it well rather than juggling seventeen other competing priorities.

DELEGATE AND ELEVATE®

LOVE / GREAT	**LIKE / GOOD**

DON'T LIKE /	**T LIKE / NOT GOOD**

Toolbox 25

Part 2: The Process

Chapter Five

EOS Overview: The Proven Process for Running Your Firm

That 20-minute Delegate and Elevate exercise you just did revealed the surface problem: You're working on too many things that someone else could do. But what if I told you there's something more profound, a secret that separates thriving law firms from struggling ones?

The Secret Successful Firms Know

Working with hundreds of law firms, I've discovered that two firms can look nearly identical on the surface. Both can have smart attorneys, solid reputations, and healthy client pipelines, yet one grows year after year while the other stays stuck. What's the difference?

It isn't talent. I've seen brilliant lawyers go broke while others, with far less pedigree, run wildly profitable firms. It isn't luck either. The pattern is too consistent for that.

The difference is invisible when you walk into the office. You won't see it in the reception area, the conference room, or even on the firm's website. But the results speak for themselves: consistent profitability, steady growth, and owners who aren't chained to their desks.

The secret? They're running on a system.

Let me tell you about Rich Hall and David Wolff, two of the founding partners at Cantor, Wolff, Nicastro & Hall, a personal injury powerhouse in Buffalo. On paper, these guys had it all figured out: over 100 years of combined experience, multiple multi-million-dollar verdicts, and a growing practice serving New York and Pennsylvania.

From the outside, they looked like the definition of success. But inside? "It was chaos," David told me without sugar-coating it.

Here's what was happening. They were working harder than ever, yet the stress never let up. Decisions got stuck at the partner level because nobody else could make them. Meetings happened when fires needed to be put out, not when strategy required planning. And David told me that every single month brought the same exhausting crisis: "Holy crap, we're growing again. Now what?"

Sound familiar? They'd scramble to reorganize, hire bodies to fill gaps, cross their fingers, and hope the wheels didn't fall off before next month's identical crisis.

Rich had been in the legal world literally "since I was in seventh grade," his words, not mine. He'd seen it all: complete chaos at some firms, slightly more organized chaos at others. He thought this was just how law firms operated. You know, like how some restaurants are disasters, and others are merely dysfunctional, but hey, that's the restaurant business.

Here's where their story gets interesting, and why I chose them for this chapter. When these guys discovered EOS, their first reaction was classic lawyer: "We can handle this ourselves."

They started self-implementing, cherry-picking tools from the book and slapping them onto their existing chaos. For a while, it helped. They got some clarity, made improvements, and stopped a few fires before they spread. But as Rich admitted later, "Our efforts were basically a partial version of EOS."

Think of it like performing surgery with half the instruments. Sure, you might not kill the patient, but you're not exactly saving them either.

Here's the kicker: Eighteen months after they stopped screwing around and fully committed to EOS, bringing in a Professional EOS Implementer® rather than trying to MacGyver it themselves, the transformation was impossible to ignore. Revenue doubled. The daily stress level got cut in half. Systems actually worked instead of existing on paper.

"My decisions now," David explained, "are trying to fix things six months from now, whereas before I was trying to fix things that happened yesterday."

So here's the intriguing question: What if the very traits that make you a brilliant lawyer are sabotaging your business? And what if the solution is simply to utilize the tools available to you to their fullest potential? Maybe you, like Rich and David, have tried to use EOS tactics without a complete understanding of how they can enhance your law firm. It's time to change that.

Why Smart Lawyers Fail at Business

Your legal training is your business weakness, a counterintuitive truth that probably pisses you off.

I know, I know. You spent three years learning to think critically, argue persuasively, and spot risk from three counties away. All fantastic skills in the courtroom. All potential business liabilities when you're trying to run a firm.

Let me break this down for you. Your perfectionism means you won't delegate anything because "nobody does it as well as I do." Your risk aversion keeps you from making the investments that actually fuel growth, like hiring an expensive but game-changing associate. Your focus on individual expertise creates a firm that can't function without you personally touching every file. And your professional skepticism makes you dismiss proven business tools as "corporate nonsense that doesn't apply to law firms."

David lived this exact nightmare. "I know I'm a very good attorney," he told me. "And for me, that comes very naturally. And I've had to work very hard at other portions of it." Translation: Being great at law was easy. Learning to run a business almost killed him.

Here's the predictable death spiral: Something goes sideways, so you work harder, taking on more yourself. Standards slip anyway because you're spread too thin. You get frustrated with your team, convince yourself you "can't find good people," and retreat even further into the "I'll just do everything myself" bunker.

It feels responsible. It feels like you're protecting quality. But it's actually the vicious cycle that burns out brilliant lawyers and turns promising firms into expensive therapy practices.

This vicious cycle was killing David and Rich. They worked harder, they took on more, their standards slipped, and they blamed the team. It felt responsible, but it was actually burning them out and limiting their growth.

So what broke the cycle? How did they go from monthly crisis mode to systematic growth in eighteen months?

The System That Changes Everything

EOS has a proven track record with thousands of successful implementations across all industries. It's not vague advice, but concrete tools. And it's designed for skeptics like you, logic-based, with measurable results.

EOS is a complete operating system for your business. Think of it like iOS for your iPhone; everything works together seamlessly. It has six integrated components, each addressing a specific business challenge. It's a proven methodology that's been developed and refined over decades. And it's an adaptable framework that works for any business, including law firms.

Why does it work for lawyers specifically? It appeals to your structured thinking. It provides the measurable results you demand. It matches how you naturally think systematically. And it creates the accountability you actually respect.

Rich saw this immediately when he read about the Visionary-Integrator model. "David fits the role of an Integrator almost to a T," he said. "It's as if *Traction* and all the other books in the EOS library were describing him as the textbook example of an Integrator." Then he looked at the Visionary role and thought, "This definitely fits my skills and my style."

The transformation EOS creates goes beyond just business metrics. It evolves owners from doers to leaders. It develops teams from dependent to independent. It shifts business growth from chaotic to systematic. And it improves life from trapped to free.

As one attorney told me, "I thought business systems were for manufacturing companies. I was wrong. EOS gave me back my life while growing my firm."

The Six Key Components That Make It Work

Here's how the Six Key Components work together to transform your firm.

Component 1: Vision

- **What it does:** Gets everyone rowing in the same direction

- **Why lawyers need it:** Prevents partner conflicts and team confusion

- **The result:** Clear decisions, aligned effort, shared purpose

Component 2: People

- **What it does:** Ensures the right people in the right seats

- **Why lawyers need it:** Solves hiring and delegation problems

- **The result:** A team you can trust, reduced micromanagement

Component 3: Data

- **What it does:** Provides visibility into firm health

- **Why lawyers need it:** Replaces gut feel with facts

- **The result:** Confident decisions, predictable outcomes

Component 4: Issues

- **What it does:** Solves problems permanently

- **Why lawyers need it:** Stops the firefighting cycle

- **The result:** Fewer recurring problems, more strategic focus

Component 5: Process

- **What it does:** Creates consistency without owner involvement

- **Why lawyers need it:** Enables successful delegation

- **The result:** Quality maintained, capacity increased

Component 6: Traction

- **What it does:** Ensures vision becomes reality

- **Why lawyers need it:** Bridges planning and execution

- **The result:** Goals achieved, momentum maintained

These Six Key Components work together like a Swiss watch. Remove any one, and the whole system breaks down. But when all six are working, the transformation is remarkable.

David described it this way: "The structure and system have led me to have so much more confidence in our overall process of where we're going and helping me understand day-to-day decisions."

Before EOS: chaos, stress, owner dependency.

After EOS: systems, growth, owner freedom.

The difference? Operating system versus operating chaos.

I can practically hear you already. "This sounds too good to be true."

That was David's first reaction too. "I am not a self-help book guy. I get great value out of them, but I did not read the book thinking that this would solve a bunch of big picture, light at the end of the tunnel, problems."

But here's what changed his mind: "Once I started reading the book, within a few chapters, I understood the big picture, and I started to see the light at the end of the tunnel. By the end of the book, I was very excited and all in."

Rich had his own moment of clarity: "I learned when I read *Reptile* by Don Keenan and David Ball that systems work. So I was sold on EOS basically by the time I got to the end of the book.

"We don't have time for this."

This is the number one objection, hands down. Mike Griffin nailed it: "I thought, Where are we going to find the time to do this?" Mike Smith echoed the same concern: "I think some people on the team were a little bit concerned about that time investment piece."

> **"We're drowning, and you want me to stop paddling to build a better boat? That's crazy. But the truth was, until we stopped and built it, we were always going to be drowning."**
> **- Constance Wannamaker**

> **"I thought we didn't have time to slow down. But not slowing down was the trap. Once we stopped and worked the system, we finally moved forward."**
> **- Lin McGraw**

Here's the brutal paradox: You don't have time NOT to do this. Marc explained it perfectly: "Any bit of change requires time commitment. And it usually takes more time. You're going to have less free time in the short term, but it's a dividend that pays off. And the sooner you do it, the sooner that dividend pays off."

When firms implement EOS, they routinely save 10 to 15 hours per week within the first 90 days. That's time you reclaim by eliminating chaos, streamlining meetings, and delegating effectively. You'll spend six days in sessions that first year, but you'll get back weeks of productive time.

"We can't afford this."

The second biggest stumbling block is money. Mike Smith was brutally honest about this concern: "I tend to look at things from the standpoint of return on investment. And this kind of thing, it's not certain... You look at the financial investment aspect of it, and you go, 'Wow, is that going to bring me

> **"It's not just the cash outlay — it's taking your whole team out of production...six days that first year, and that's not nothing. That was definitely a concern."**
> **-Mike Smith**

three times, four times, 10 times, 100 times? What is that going to bring me back?'"

Let's talk real numbers, because this isn't cheap. Yes, hiring an implementer runs $30,000 to $50,000 for the first year. And yes, you have to take your entire leadership team out of production for five or six days during implementation. As Mike put it, "That's not nothing, for sure."

What you can't afford is the cost you're already paying in stress, employee turnover, missed opportunities, and your own sanity. Mike discovered this when his revenue was up 40 percent, but he was taking home less money than the year before. The financial return on getting your systems right isn't hypothetical; it's measurable. Within 18 months of implementation, Mike's firm had doubled revenue and dramatically improved profit margins.

"We're too unique for a generic system."

Every law firm believes this. Hell, every business believes this. The truth? Businesses are 80 percent similar, 20 percent unique. EOS handles the 80 percent; you customize the 20 percent.

Rich had worked at a large personal injury firm where he'd helped build processes and procedures from six lawyers up to 30. He'd seen firsthand how the right systems could manage explosive growth. When they found EOS, he and David "built the systems around my knowledge base, but in a manner that we thought addressed the shortcomings of their previous firm."

They didn't throw out what made them unique. They built on what worked and fixed what didn't. Revolutionary concept, I know.

"This will make us feel corporate."

This one makes me laugh. Good systems don't change culture; they enhance what makes you special. Boutique firms using EOS are still boutique, just better run. Think of it like upgrading from a flip phone to an iPhone. You're still you, just more capable.

David nailed the real transformation: "Since we implemented the system, now when we have a disagreement amongst the partners in what should be done... We're quicker on decisions. We're not wasting time... People are understanding their roles. And that is saving a lot of time."

So let me leave you with the clincher question: What's riskier: trying a proven system or continuing to wing it?

What Happens Next?

Whether you're new to EOS or have been running on the system for years, here are a few reminders and best practices for the implementation journey as a law firm.

First, don't expect overnight miracles. Full implementation typically takes 18 to 24 months. But you'll see progress almost immediately. Each quarter builds on the last, with clear milestones and measurable improvements along the way. You can also set the pace. Some firms move quickly, others take it slower. EOS adapts to your capacity, not the other way around.

Second, make sure you know where you're going and get your team aligned around that vision before you do anything to try to get there. If you look at the EOS Model, you'll notice Vision sits right at the top. There's a reason for that. You certainly won't get where you're going if you don't know where that is. Vision is the foundation everything else builds on; it's how you get everyone in your organization 100 percent on the same page with where you're headed and how you plan to get there.

But here's something EOS gets right that most business systems get wrong: vision without traction is hallucination. You can have the clearest picture of your future imaginable, but if you don't have the discipline and accountability to execute on it, you've just got a really nice daydream. That's why EOS pairs Vision with Traction, the tools and pulses that take your vision down to the ground and make it real, day in and day out.

Mike Smith experienced this transformation. "We had all these reports, but they never told me anything useful," he said about his pre-EOS days. "Revenue looked good, expenses looked normal, but I still had no idea if we were actually making money." Vision gave him the clarity to see what numbers actually mattered and why. Traction gave him the discipline to do something about it.

What will you discover in the Vision phase?

- Immediate clarity about what you're actually building.

- Team buy-in because people want to be part of something bigger than just "making money."

- Decision confidence with clear criteria for tough choices.

- Energy renewal as Vision reignites passion for your work.

David summed up the transformation: "The structure and system have led me to have so much more confidence in our overall process of where we're going and helping me understand day-to-day decisions. It really makes a big difference."

EOS is the system that transforms firms like Rich and David's from chaos to clarity. It's not about theory. It's not about luck. It's about building the discipline and systems that make Vision possible. And once you see how it works, you'll never look at your firm the same way again.

The Moment of Truth

You now know the secret. The question is: What are you going to do with it?

Vision sits at the top of the EOS Model because it aligns everything else. It's the easiest to start because it doesn't require major operational changes, just clarity. And it provides immediate benefit because once you know where you're going, every decision becomes easier.

What's different about EOS Vision? It's not a corporate mission statement gathering dust on the wall. It's not the owner's private dream that nobody else shares. It's not wishful thinking without substance.

EOS Vision is a real picture of your future. It's a shared vision that genuinely inspires your team. It's a concrete plan with specific milestones you can measure. And paired with Traction, it's a vision you'll actually achieve.

Stop trying to build a business without a blueprint. In the next chapter, I'm going to show you exactly how to create a vision so clear and compelling that your team will be excited to help you build it.

EOS Vision is a real picture of your future.

Chapter Six

Building the Firm You Actually Want

You're ready to build your vision. But first, let me show you what real vision looks like in action, and why most law firms are doing it completely wrong.

The Power of True Vision

Remember Constance Wannamaker? When you met her, she was running a $20 million immigration firm with 100 employees that looked successful from the outside but felt like barely controlled chaos on the inside. Every choice, big or small, ran through her desk. Her staff members weren't failing; they were waiting for everything.

"For me, as a visionary, I'm spouting out all this stuff that I wanted everybody to do," Constance explained. "Accountability was an issue. We didn't have a good structure to figure out 'Where are we going, what do we want to do, and how do we get there?'"

Think about that for a second. A $20 million firm with 100 employees, and nobody except Constance knew where they were headed. Sound familiar?

When her EOS Implementer suggested creating a shared vision, Constance's first thought was probably the same as yours: "Do we really need to sit around wordsmithing mission statements?" Like most attorneys, she assumed "vision" meant corporate fluff, something you put on your website to make clients feel warm and fuzzy, not something that would actually change how her firm operated.

Her team was skeptical too. These were busy people drowning in case files, not sitting in conference rooms talking about feelings and the future. They had real work to do, thank you very much.

But here's where the story gets interesting. As Constance worked through the Vision/Traction Organizer® with her leadership team, something shifted. For the first time, she finally had the vision clearly laid out in a way that helped her and her team make decisions. She saw clearly who were the right people that belonged at her firm. She also got excited about truly identifying her cause: to create new citizens by practicing immigration law. That purpose ignited her team in a way revenue targets never could.

The breakthrough moment came when they realized they weren't just processing paperwork, they were creating new citizens. They weren't just filling out forms; they were making the American dream come true. That wasn't just a job; it was a mission worth the fight.

Compare that to what most firms call "vision": generic mission statements about "providing quality legal services to our clients" (revolutionary!), pretty plaques on the wall that no one can recite, or worse, the owner's private dream that he never speaks aloud. None of that provides alignment. None of it helps your team make better decisions. And none of it inspires anyone to work late on a Friday.

Real vision is different. It's a concrete picture of your future firm that everyone shares. It's a destination, not a decoration. And when the work gets hard, and it will, it's the source of energy that keeps people pushing forward.

Real vision is a concrete picture of your future firm that everyone shares.

"Before vision," Constance told me, "we were just managing a law practice." After creating vision? "We were building something meaningful."

The Two Types of Lawyers Who Can Build Vision

When it comes to building vision, not all attorneys are created equal. After working with hundreds of lawyers, there are two types that can create a compelling vision that actually inspires teams. All the others are just going through the motions.

Cause-Based Lawyers: Driven by Purpose and Justice

There are attorneys like Constance, lawyers who entered the profession as a calling. They're fighting for something bigger than themselves, and they usually have a personal connection to the injustice they're now battling.

- Immigration attorneys who are immigrants themselves, seeking to create the American dream for others.

- Personal injury attorneys who were injured or watched family members get hurt and saw how the system tried to screw them.

- Trust and estate lawyers who watched families get cheated in probate and decided someone needed to fight back.

Their vision focuses on amplifying impact, serving more people, and fighting bigger battles. Think "making the American dream come true for 500,000 people" or "protecting 10,000 families from nursing home abuse."

These lawyers measure success in lives changed, justice delivered, and wrongs made right. They want to build something that can create a massive positive impact, something that serves their cause at scale while also paying the bills.

Entrepreneurial Lawyers:
Entrepreneurs First, Lawyers Second

Then there are the attorneys who see their legal degree as the foundation for building something bigger. They didn't go to law school to practice law; they went to law school to build an empire that happens to involve legal services.

They get excited about scalable business models, multiple revenue streams, and market domination. Their vision focuses on growth, expansion, and business success. Think "the go-to law firm for Series A tech companies" or "the premier employment law firm in Texas with 50 attorneys and $50M in revenue."

These lawyers measure success in enterprise value, market share, and business metrics. They want to build something that can eventually run without them, something they can scale, systematize, and potentially sell for eight figures.

What Both Types Share

Whether you're driven by entrepreneurial growth or a meaningful cause, certain foundational elements remain the same.

- **They want something bigger** than just putting food on the table and paying off law school loans.

- **They're willing to do the work** to implement systems that support their bigger vision.

- **They can inspire others** with a vision that team members want to join.

- **They have a growth mindset** and understand that a bigger vision requires better systems.

The Third Type, We Can't Help

There's a third type of attorney we run into all the time: the "no vision" lawyer. When you ask them what they want to build, they shrug and say, "I don't know. I just want a law firm."

Here's the brutal reality: If your vision doesn't even inspire you, there's no way I can use it to motivate your team. People don't quit their jobs to be part of something generic. They don't work extra hours for "just a law firm." They don't stick around during challenging times for "we provide quality legal services."

If your vision doesn't even inspire you, there's no way I can use it to motivate your team.

So if you're thinking, "I just want to practice law and make money," this chapter probably isn't for you. Maybe try accounting instead. Or better yet, work for somebody else.

Why Lawyers Struggle with Vision

If vision is so powerful, why do so many attorneys resist it like it's a root canal?

It Feels "Soft": Lawyers prefer concrete over conceptual. You like facts, evidence, and measurable outcomes. Vision feels touchy-feely, like something you'd find in a corporate retreat full of trust falls and team-building exercises where everyone pretends to care about synergy.

It Sounds Corporate: Most attorneys got into law to practice law, not to become business executives with corner offices and buzzword-heavy PowerPoint presentations. Vision gets associated with big business, something that doesn't fit the professional services world, where you genuinely care about your clients.

Past Disappointment: Many firms have tried strategic planning before. They spent days in conference rooms, created beautiful binders with mission statements, and watched them gather dust next to last year's strategic plan. Why would this time be different?

Time Pressure: "We're too busy putting out fires to think about the future." Sound familiar? When you're drowning in daily crises, long-term thinking feels like a luxury you can't afford. Like taking a vacation while your house is burning down.

The Perfectionist Trap: Lawyers want the perfect vision before they start. They analyze every word, debate every nuance, and end up in paralysis by analysis. Meanwhile, firms with "good enough" vision are already executing and improving while you're still wordsmithing.

But here's why vision matters more for law firms than other businesses:

- Professional services are harder to differentiate. When every lawyer promises "quality legal services" and "zealous advocacy," vision is what actually sets you apart.

- Partnership dynamics require alignment. Multiple decision-makers need to be pulling in the same direction, or you'll tear the firm apart faster than a bad prenup.

- Top talent wants to be part of something bigger. The best people don't just want good pay; they want meaningful work that doesn't make them question their life choices.

- Client expectations have evolved. Clients choose firms with clear direction and purpose, not just technical competence and fancy letterhead.

The cost of no vision? Without vision, every decision becomes a committee debate. With vision, most decisions become obvious.

The Clarity Break: Your Vision Discovery Tool

Before you can create a shared vision with your team, you need individual clarity. And I'm sorry, but you can't get that clarity while you're buried in daily operations, answering emails between hearings, and eating lunch at your desk while reviewing briefs.

What Is a Clarity Break?

EOS developed the concept of a Clarity Break as a way to completely disconnect from daily chaos and think freely about what you actually want. Think of it like this: You're rowing a boat as fast as you can, focused entirely on the next stroke. A Clarity Break is when you finally stop rowing long enough to look up and ask, "Wait, where the hell am I going? And is this even the right boat to get me there?"

For Constance, this kind of thinking was a turning point. Before EOS, she had been stuck in reactive mode, answering questions, managing crises, and being the bottleneck for everything. When she finally stepped back to think about the bigger picture, she realized she'd been running on autopilot. The firm was growing, but it wasn't designed to give her or her team the future they wanted.

How to Take a Clarity Break

There's no magic formula for how or where. Some people grab a notebook and sit in a coffee shop, watching the world go by (and no, scrolling Instagram doesn't count). Others head to a park, a hiking trail, or even the zoo, anywhere they can get out of their normal environment and let their minds wander so they can think.

A few block out half a day at church or in meditation, if that's where their mind can settle. The key is not the setting, but the disconnection. No email, no calls, no "just checking in" with the office. If you're scrolling on your phone, it's not a Clarity Break; it's just procrastination with a fancy name.

Make your Clarity Break however long it needs to be to actually clear your head. Spend an hour between hearings. Take a half-day. If you need it, take a whole day. Your brain just needs time to stop running the daily script of crisis management. I find that some of the most powerful clarity moments happen on vacation, when you've unplugged long enough that your brain finally stops automatically thinking about what's waiting in your inbox.

When I first started doing Clarity Breaks, I was convinced I was doing them all wrong. I would sit down, theoretically to think clearly (it's in the name, right?), and all I could do was make page after page of lists. Call back that client. Deal with that team member issue. Pick up salmon for dinner. I told a member of my team that I felt like I needed to clean out my email inbox before I could start. Her reply? "You'll never take a Clarity Break at this rate."

But what I learned was I needed to get all the minutia out of my head. All those little things that distracted me anytime I tried to think about anything larger than where I was going to get lunch. Until I emptied my brain by writing it all down, I couldn't quiet my mind enough to have coherent and productive thoughts. And that is where the magic starts to happen.

Does it feel like a waste of time to make the lists? It did until I realized that was the price of admission. I also learned that the more often I took Clarity Breaks, the less time it took to ready my mind. Because that is when the real work begins, and you can finally ask yourself the big questions about the future of your firm instead of obsessing about your inbox.

Questions Worth Asking

What should you think about on a Clarity Break? Anything you want, but a lot of people start with the big picture.

- If the world had no limitations, what would my ideal life look like in ten years?

- What kind of firm would serve that life?

- If I could serve ten times more clients, what would that look like?

- What injustice am I uniquely positioned to fight?

- How do I want to be remembered?

- What would I do if money weren't a concern?

- If I could wave a magic wand and fix one thing in my field, what would it be?

Those aren't just thought experiments. They're the raw material for vision. Constance's answers to these questions weren't about revenue targets or headcount. They were about impact: creating more citizens, changing more lives, and helping families achieve the American dream. Once she articulated that, the rest of her firm's vision snapped into place.

When Individual Clarity Isn't Enough

Of course, vision can't live in the owner's head forever. At some point, you need your leadership team's perspective. Sometimes their ideas unlock blocks you didn't even know you had. Many times, they see opportunities you've been too close to notice. And when the vision becomes a shared product, it's no longer "my dream," it's "our future." That shift changes everything about buy-in and execution.

But here's the catch: You can't outsource vision completely. If the owner isn't inspired by the vision, nobody else will be. And not every team is ready to have this conversation. The hard truth is that the people who got you here may not be the ones to take you there. Some won't think strategically. Some will resist change. Some will leave when they realize they don't want to play at a higher level.

You can't outsource vision completely.

That's painful, but it's also part of growth. And honestly? If someone's not excited about building something meaningful, do you really want them on your team?

The V/TO®: Your Vision Blueprint

Attorneys love paper. Contracts, pleadings, briefs, you can stack them to the ceiling. But when it comes to charting the future of their firm, most lawyers don't write anything down. They carry it in their heads like some kind of mystical business plan, or, worse, assume everyone magically knows what they want.

That's why EOS gives you the Vision/Traction Organizer® (for the V/TO, see pages 64 & 65).[1] Think of it as your vision blueprint. Two simple pages that capture everything important about your firm's future. It's not a thick binder destined for a shelf (looking at you, strategic planning consultants). It's a living document you revisit at a minimum every quarter to align the entire team, literally putting everyone on the same page.

The V/TO consists of eight seemingly simple questions. What is/are your:

1. Core Values - These are a handful of guiding principles that define your culture.

2. Core Focus - Why you exist as an organization and what you are better at doing than anybody else in the world.

3. 10-Year Target - Your big, long-range goal.

4. Marketing Strategy - Identifies your target market, what makes you unique to them, and how you set expectations.

5. 3-Year Picture - What will your firm be in three years? Not just revenue, but paint the full picture.

6. 1-Year Plan - What you are going to accomplish this year.

7. Rocks - These lay out what you will accomplish in the next 90 days.

8. Issues - What are the problems you need to solve in your firm to move it forward?

When Constance first worked through her V/TO, she realized how much of her "vision" had never been spoken aloud. It was floating around in her head, half-formed, impossible for her team to execute. Once it was written down, the fog lifted. Suddenly, everyone could see where they were going.

---

1. The complete V/TO is available to download at http://eosworldwide.com/VTO-download .

For Constance's team, this was the aha moment. The vision was inspiring and energizing. She was also able to get her whole team aligned around their BHAG (Big Hairy Audacious Goal) or the 10-Year Target, as EOS calls it, which for them is "Help create 30,000 new citizens a year." For her team, that is more than a number; it enables them to see the impact they are making, and that is inspiring.

"We spent a lot of time on it. We thought initially, well, we have to pick a number. Yeah, well, we have to pick a number, but that's not what gets people excited." So while her 10-Year Target contains a number that enables them to measure it, what really matters is creating citizens.

The 3-Year Picture was the first time her team could truly see themselves in the future of the firm. Instead of vague hopes about "getting bigger," it described specific numbers, specific roles, and the specific culture they wanted to build. Everyone knew what mattered most this year, what had to get done this quarter, and what would wait. Suddenly, the firm wasn't just moving, it was moving in the same direction.

Creating Your V/TO: Self-Implementation vs. Professional Guidance

You can't build a Vision/Traction Organizer in the margins of your day, squeezing it in between court appearances, client calls, and frantically trying to respond to that set of 'roggs due by the end of the day. If you try, you'll end up with half-baked statements nobody believes in and a team that's more confused than inspired.

Some firms choose to self-implement, which means taking two to three days away from the firm, completely disconnected from email, phones, and daily operations, and working through all eight questions on your own with your leadership team. Block the time, go off-site, bring flip chart paper and markers, and commit to doing the work. Many firms have successfully built their V/TO this way.

The other option is to hire an EOS Implementer to guide you through the process. This takes roughly the same amount of time, typically three full days spread over about two months, but it tends to get better results. An Implementer brings an outside perspective, keeps you from common pitfalls, and holds you accountable for completing the work. They've seen the patterns that trip up law firms and can steer you away from them before you waste time going down the wrong path.

Many firms start with self-implementation, make some progress, and then ultimately hire an Implementer when they realize they need help refining what they've built or getting truly aligned as a team. There's no shame in that approach. The important thing is that you do the work, whether on your own or with professional guidance.

Either way, the key is complete disconnection from daily operations. Phones off. Laptops closed. No, "Just checking email really quickly." This is about future-building, and it deserves your full attention. Come ready to think big, be brutally honest, and leave the "but we can't because..." objections at the door.

The Most Common Pitfall When Attorneys Self-Implement

Most of you know that Core Values are three to seven guiding principles that are the foundation for the culture of your firm. However, I can't tell you how many lawyers I have seen dismiss Core Values as "worthless" or "BS" or "something that consultant made us do." And all of this is true *if* Core Values are done improperly.

There is a great Harvard Business Review article by Patrick Lencioni called "Make Your Values Mean Something."[2] In it, he talks about how to use Core Values, weaving them into every part of your company to identify the "Right People." This is mistake number 1. Law firms think they can paste their brand spankin' new Core Values up on a wall somewhere and they are done. That is only the very beginning. You have to live them. And that is hard to do day in and day out. Most people give up. I heard a great phrase recently: "If it hasn't cost you money, it isn't really a Core Value." Living your Core Values means making hard decisions that cost you money because the Values are more important than the cash.

Lencioni also discussed the different types of values. You all know Core Values, but what about Accidental (ones that developed and you didn't even realize it), Aspirational (ones that you want to be true, but really aren't), and Permission-to-Play values (basic expectations). The last two are the traps I see firms falling into the most. They pick something generic like Integrity because everybody wants an honest lawyer, right? First, if you

---

2. Lencioni, Partick M. (2002). "Make Your Values Mean Something," Harvard Business Review, R0207J

have to say you're honest, most people doubt that you are. Second, isn't it a given that you hire honest employees? Is it really necessary to state out loud that you do basic employee vetting to make sure you aren't hiring ax murderers and embezzlers? That is Permission-to-Play.

And what about Aspirational values? These are things like adding "Work Life Balance" as a value when you expect everybody but Partners to bill 2500 hours a year. They mean well, but it directly conflicts with their billable goals. And we all know that hitting billable goals is more important than anything else. Therefore, work-life balance becomes aspirational and devalues everything else you have said.

Special Considerations for Law Firms

Law firms have a few unique wrinkles in this process. Regulatory compliance is always in play; your vision can be big, but it can't violate Bar rules or ethics requirements. Partnerships add another layer of complexity; sometimes you'll need to sort out the partners' personal visions before you can align on a firm-wide one.

Don't forget your cause. If you're a cause-based lawyer, your business vision should amplify the impact you care about most. Finally, always ask: How will this vision improve client experience and outcomes? Because if it doesn't serve your clients better, what's the point?

Making Vision Stick: Shared By All

Once you've answered all eight questions and your V/TO is complete, you might think you're done. You're not. You've created a vision that your leadership team shares and believes in. Now you need to share it with everyone in your organization.

This is what EOS calls "Shared By All," and it's the second discipline within the Vision Component®.

If you have 25 people in your organization, all 25 need to see that vision, understand your plan, and want to be part of it. Not just your leadership team. Everyone. The receptionist needs to understand where the firm is going. The newest paralegal needs to know what you stand for. Every single person should be able to articulate the Core Values and know how their role contributes to your 10-Year Target.

Here's how you make that happen: Quarterly State of the Company addresses. I call them State of the Firm Addresses and then refer to them as SOFAs.

Every 90 days, get everyone in a room and share where the firm is headed. Go over your V/TO again, all eight questions. Celebrate wins from the past quarter. Be transparent about challenges and honest about what needs to improve.

This isn't a boring corporate presentation where the owner drones on for an hour while people check their phones. This is energy. This is connection. This is reminding everyone why they show up to work and what they're building together.

When you consistently share your vision this way, something magical happens. All those people start rowing in one direction. They're not just executing tasks; they're working toward a shared future they helped create (or at least understand and believe in). They make better decisions because they know what the firm stands for. They stay longer because they're part of something meaningful.

Before Constance implemented Shared By All, her vision lived in her head and maybe in her leadership team's minds. After? "Everybody can see it too. This is what we're going to do. This is where we're going." Her entire 100-person firm aligned around creating new citizens, not just processing immigration paperwork.

When Vision Reveals Team Gaps

Sometimes, vision reveals team gaps, a fact most attorneys don't want to hear. When you set a higher bar, not everyone will be able, or willing, to reach it. Some current team members won't fit the vision. Others will resist change. A few will leave when they realize they don't want to play at a higher level.

That hurts. But the flip side is that vision also shows you who can grow with you. Those are the people you invest in because they'll become the backbone of the firm you're building.

Constance saw this firsthand when she clarified her vision. "When we started doing the weekly L10s and getting the issues out, and everybody had their Rocks and their to-dos, it was interesting to see who got what done," she told me.

But more importantly, the vision process revealed who was really aligned with the firm's direction and who wasn't. Some people leaned in harder. Others eventually self-selected out. Painful, yes. Necessary, absolutely.

Vision sets the foundation. You now know where you're going, what you stand for, and what kind of firm you're building. But vision without the right people is just a waste of your time and effort.

The right people follow a compelling vision. They are drawn to firms that stand for something more than billable hours and profit margins. Vision aligns you, your leadership team, and your staff around the same destination. It creates accountability because everyone knows what they're contributing to and how success is defined. And it builds retention because people stay longer when they're part of something bigger than themselves.

> **The vision process revealed who was really aligned with the firm's direction and who wasn't.**

This raises the harder questions, though. Do you have the right people on your team? Are they in the right seats? Are they performing at the level your vision requires? And, just as important, are they growing with the firm or holding it back?

Constance learned this lesson the hard way when her longtime chief of staff had to leave the firm. "She left. It was not a good break," Constance told me. The person who had been with her from the beginning, promoted from intern to Chief of Staff to Integrator, wasn't the right person to help execute the vision they'd built.

"The person I have now is a really highly experienced, very high-level guy. Is he perfect? No. But he gets shit done, and he's not afraid to say, well, I fucked that up, or that was my fault."

That's the difference between someone who fits your vision and someone who doesn't. Vision without the right team is just wishful thinking.

> **Vision without the right team is just wishful thinking.**

In the next chapter, I'll show you exactly how to build a team you can finally trust, one that shares your vision and can execute it without you micromanaging every detail.

VISION/TRACTION ORGANIZER®

ORGANIZATION NAME: ______________________

VISION

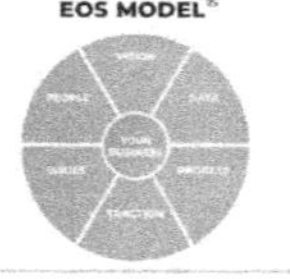

CORE VALUES	1. 2. 3. 4. 5.		3-YEAR PICTURE
CORE FOCUS	Purpose/Cause/Passion: Our Niche:		Future Date: Revenue: Profit: Measurables: What Does It Look Like? • • • • • • •
10-YEAR TARGET	_______________________ _______________________		• • • •

MARKETING STRATEGY	Target Market/"The List":
	
	3 Uniques: 1.
	              2.
	              3.
	Proven Process:
	
	Guarantee:		

VISION/TRACTION ORGANIZER®

ORGANIZATION NAME: ______________________

VISION

CORE VALUES	1. 2. 3. 4. 5.	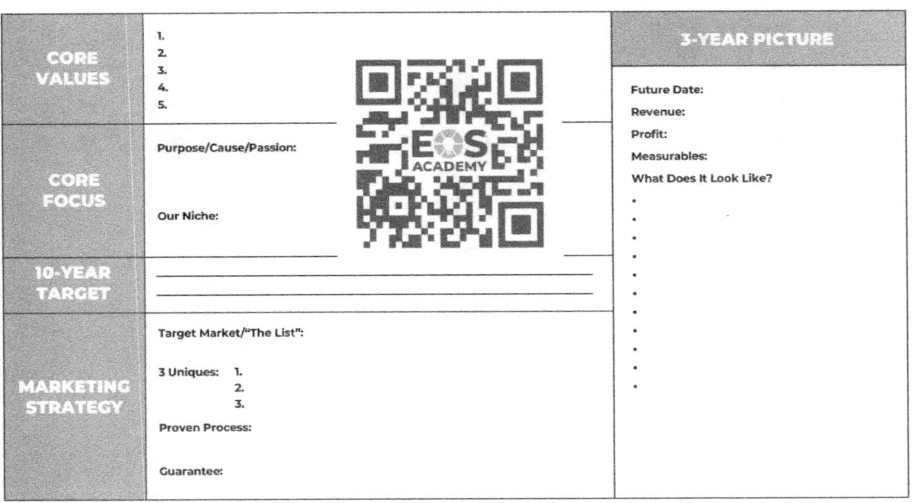	**3-YEAR PICTURE**
CORE FOCUS	Purpose/Cause/Passion: Our Niche:		Future Date: Revenue: Profit: Measurables: What Does It Look Like? • • • • • • • • • •
10-YEAR TARGET			
MARKETING STRATEGY	Target Market/"The List": 3 Uniques: 1. 2. 3. Proven Process: Guarantee:		

Chapter Seven

How to Build a Team You Can Finally Trust

You have your vision. Now comes the most challenging part: building a team that can execute it without you micromanaging every detail.

The Million-Dollar Plateau

Lynn St. Louis had a problem most lawyers would kill for: She couldn't break through $2 million in revenue. This wasn't because she wasn't talented or didn't have clients. Her estate planning firm in Washington was doing well by most measures. Good work. Happy clients. Steady income. Nice profit.

But stuck. Completely, frustratingly stuck.

"I felt like I was at the million to two million dollar range for longer than I wanted to be," she told me. "I didn't have a great way to run the firm. I didn't know what I didn't know."

She'd followed the law school playbook, you know, the one that teaches you to build a firm based on your own heroic efforts. Work the cases. Close the deals. Be the genius everyone depends on. It works great until you hit your capacity ceiling and realize you've built a very expensive job for yourself.

Lynn knew she needed help. She'd tried bringing in a Chief Operating Officer years earlier through a recruiter. "Totally failed," she said flatly. No structure. No framework. Just the vague idea that having another person would magically solve everything.

Sound familiar?

What Law Firms Actually Sell

Law firms are different from every other business. You're not selling widgets. You're selling people's brains and expertise. Every client interaction depends on your team's thinking. Clients hire people they trust, not just firm names on a door. This means your people are everything. Not your fancy office. Not your marketing budget. Not your technology stack. *Your people*.

When you have the wrong people or the right people in the wrong seats, everything breaks. Client service deteriorates. Your best employees get frustrated and leave. You spend your time managing drama instead of growing the firm. You wake up at 3 a.m., wondering if you'll ever get your life back.

When you have the right people in the right seats, magic happens. Work flows. Clients rave. Your team solves problems without you. You actually sleep through the night.

The challenge is figuring out who's who, and then doing something about it.

Right People, Right Seats: The Framework That Changes Everything

EOS has a deceptively simple tool for this: The People Analyzer. It answers two questions about every person on your team.

1. **Right People:** Do they share your Core Values?

2. **Right Seats:** Do they Get it, Want it, and have the Capacity (GWC®) for their seat?

Let me break this down because it's more powerful than it sounds. Remember those Core Values from your V/TO in Chapter 6? You use those to define the Right People. But before we can decide if somebody is sitting in the Right Seat, we have to define the seat. EOS does this using the Accountability Chart.

The Accountability Chart®: Structure That Actually Makes Sense

Most law firms go wrong by creating an org chart showing who reports to whom, putting everyone's name in a little box, and calling it a day. That's not structure. That's a reporting relationship diagram.

The Accountability Chart is different[1]. It shows major functions first, people second.

At the leadership level, most law firms need these functions:

- **Integrator:** The person who leads and manages the entire leadership team and is accountable for executing the business plan

- **Sales/Marketing:** Find prospects and turn them into clients.

- **Operations:** Delivery of legal services

- **Finance:** Money, billing, collections, HR, IT. I think of this as all the Shared Services.

Notice I didn't list job titles. I listed what needs to happen in your firm. There is one more that most firms have, but isn't absolutely necessary:

- **Visionary:** The person with big ideas and future vision (usually the founding partner)

Once you've identified your major functions, you need to crystallize exactly what each seat does. Not a 37-bullet-point job description that no one reads. Five roles. That's it. What are the five most important things this person must deliver to succeed in their seat? These aren't tasks like "answer emails" or "attend meetings." They're the core responsibilities or outcomes that define success.

There's One More Seat

I've saved the most controversial seat for last, and it's one that makes law firm partners deeply uncomfortable: the Owner's Box.

---

1. To learn more about the Accountability Chart, go to www.EOSWorldwide.com/Accountability-Chart-Download

Here's the thing most attorneys don't understand (or refuse to accept): owning equity in a firm and having a seat on the leadership team are two completely different things. The Owner's Box sits above The Accountability Chart, separate from it. It's where shareholders, partners, and owners reside. And here's the part that makes lawyers twitch: being in the Owner's Box does not automatically entitle you to a seat on the leadership team.

Let that sink in for a moment.

You can own 30 percent of a law firm and not be the Visionary. You can have your name on the door and not be the Integrator. You can have been there since day one and not run Operations. Ownership is about equity. Leadership team seats are about function. They're earned through capability, not bought through partnership.

I watch this play out constantly. A firm has four equity partners, so they assume they need four people on the leadership team. Or worse, they create fake seats to make sure everyone has a title. "Well, Bob is a partner, so he has to be on the leadership team somewhere." No. Bob has to be in the right seat based on what the business needs, or Bob needs to stay in the Owner's Box and let someone else do the job.

The Owner's Box has real power, but it's a different kind of power. Owners set the overall direction of the firm. They make decisions about profit distribution, major capital expenditures, bringing on new partners, and yes, whether the people in those top leadership seats are truly performing. If the Integrator isn't doing their job? The Owner's Box can fire them. If the Visionary is taking the firm in an unwanted or overly risky direction? The Owner's Box can make that call.

Owners set the overall direction of the firm.

I saw this play out beautifully with a firm you've already met out of Buffalo. They have three partners: Rich, David, and Joe. Rich is the Visionary. David is the Integrator. But Joe? Joe wasn't in a leadership seat, and he was struggling with that. He felt like he wasn't in control, like he didn't have power. The firm was having trouble getting him fully bought in because nobody had explained how the Owner's Box works.

When we clarified the structure, everything changed. David put it this way: "At the end of the day, the Owner's Box decides if I'm not doing my job as the Integrator. The owners make that call. I can get fired as the Integrator." That realization was huge for Joe. He understood that he absolutely has power and control. It's just a different type of control than running day-to-day operations.

David called it a "game changer." Joe finally understood that sitting in the Owner's Box isn't a consolation prize. It's the ultimate accountability mechanism.

Partners assume that their equity stake guarantees them a leadership role. It doesn't. What it guarantees is a voice in how the firm is governed and a share of the profits, but operationally running the firm? That goes to whoever is best suited for each seat, partner or not.

And yes, this means a non-equity employee, possibly even a non-attorney, might be better suited for a leadership seat than one of your founding partners. I know that's hard to hear. But if your goal is building a firm that functions at a high level instead of one that protects egos, you need to separate ownership from operation.

The Owner's Box isn't about being sidelined. It's about being elevated to the place where you hold the entire leadership team accountable for results. That's real power. Most partners just don't recognize it until someone explains it to them.

Evaluating Your Team: The People Analyzer in Action

EOS has developed a tool called The People Analyzer (page 77) to help you pull all this information into one place so you can easily evaluate your team. Simply put your Core Values across the top, followed by the initials for GWC. Write employee names down the side and start evaluating. It is a quick and easy way to see who can stay and who needs to go.

A lot of my clients are very visual, so I've borrowed a grid from Chad Gono that maps the different types of employees. I call it the Puppy Graph.

Top Right, Right Person, Right Seat: These people share your values AND excel at their jobs. You know them. They make your life easier. They solve problems instead of creating them. We call them **Stars**. Invest in them. Promote them. Give them opportunities to grow. And stop taking them for granted while you're busy managing problem people.

Bottom Left, Wrong Person, Wrong Seat: Also easy to identify, these people don't fit your culture, AND they're not good at their jobs. We call them **Rats** (Star spelled backwards) because they are the complete opposite. Help them exit immediately. There's no path forward here.

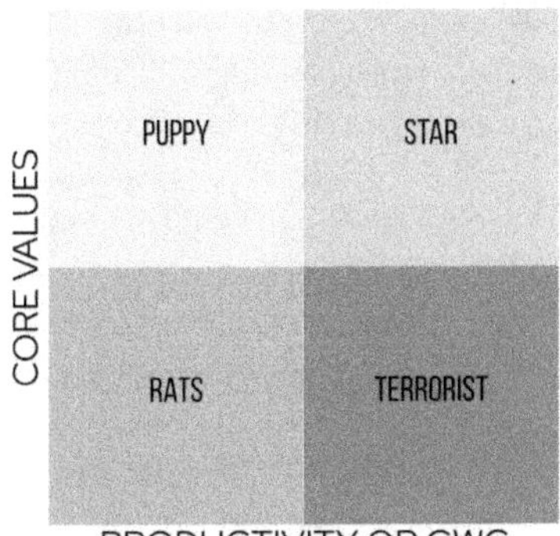

Top Left, Right Person, Wrong Seat: We call them Puppies. Why? They're cute, they're sweet, they make everybody feel all warm and fuzzy inside, but they piddle all over the floor. They share your values, but they don't have the skills for the job. They're drowning in their current role. Maybe your detail-oriented paralegal is trying to do business development and dying inside, or perhaps your brilliant litigator is stuck doing transactional work and bored out of their mind. The good news is that you might have another seat where they'd be a Star. Move them before you lose them. If you don't have the right seat for them, help them find it somewhere else. Don't keep Puppies in the wrong seat just because you like them. It's not fair to them or your firm.

Bottom Right, Wrong Person, Right Seat: They're productive, maybe even brilliant. They bill more hours than anyone. They bring in big clients. They win cases. But they don't share your values, and that's poison.

You're afraid to address their behavior because you need their production. You need their book of business or their technical expertise. So you make excuses. You tolerate the partner who screams at staff, the associate who takes credit for everyone else's work, or the rainmaker who treats people like disposable commodities. You rationalize that they're "just intense" or "that's how they show they care about quality." They are effectively holding you hostage. And that's why we call them **Terrorists**.

While you're being held hostage, your Stars start looking for the exit. Because your best people have options; they'll tolerate it for a while out of loyalty, but eventually they'll leave. And when they do, they'll cite "better opportunities," but the real reason is they're tired of watching you protect the Terrorist.

Every day you keep a Terrorist, you're teaching your entire team that your Core Values are just nice words on the wall. That production trumps culture. That bringing in money means you can treat people however you want.

I've seen firms lose three Stars trying to avoid dealing with one Terrorist. The math never works. When you finally address it (give them a genuine chance to change with clear expectations, then exit them if they don't), the entire firm exhales. Your Stars stop updating their resumes. And that revenue you were afraid of losing? It usually gets replaced faster than you think.

The hardest part of this exercise isn't doing the assessment. It's doing something with what you learn.

The Visionary/Integrator Split: The Distinction That Changes Everything

Most law firm owners are trying to be both Visionary and Integrator while also practicing law. This is the fastest path to burnout I know.

The Visionary has big ideas, sees the future, loves new possibilities, and is terrible at follow-through. They're creative, entrepreneurial, great with relationships, and would rather die than manage the details of a project plan.

The Integrator makes things happen. They're good at managing people, processes, and day-to-day operations. They love execution and accountability. They're usually terrible at sitting still and dreaming about the future.

You need both roles filled. One person cannot do both roles well. Period.

Lynn's Integration Revolution

Back to Lynn. She spent six months trying to implement EOS with just her marketing director. They read the book. They thought they were doing Rocks, Accountability Charts, and all the tools.

"We were just clueless," she admitted. "We did not know what we were doing at all. Honestly, I don't know how anybody could implement EOS without the teacher."

So she hired an EOS Implementer. They built a real Accountability Chart. They did People Analyzer assessments on everyone. They identified the seats they needed versus the people they had.

And here's where it gets interesting: Lynn discovered she had remarkably low turnover. Most firms implementing EOS lose 30–40 percent of their people. Lynn? Almost no one left.

"Most people have been with me for five years now," she said. "We did not have turnover."

Why? Because she had the Right People. They'd been with her through thick and thin. They shared her values. The problem wasn't the people. It was the seats.

Lynn's legal manager was in the wrong role. Her marketing director seat exceeded the occupant's skills. But the biggest revelation? She needed an Integrator.

This year, Lynn hired Randie, an experienced integrator who'd worked with EOS before. She was someone who could take all the operational stuff off Lynn's plate and make it work.

The impact was immediate.

"Right away," Lynn said when I asked how quickly she noticed the difference. "She's just making all sorts of differences. She's HR, she's great with people, great with one-on-ones, making people feel like a part of the firm."

Then Lynne said something that stopped me: "I'm more of a 'get your job done, please' type person. She is more of a 'bringing out the best in people' person."

That's the Visionary/Integrator split in action, folks. Lynn can finally be who she naturally is instead of trying to be everything to everyone.

The results? Lynn's firm has gone from being stuck at $2 million to over $3 million this year and is targeting $5 million. Not because she's working more. Because she finally has the right structure with the right people in the right seats.

"It's actually kind of a relief," she told me. "That I'm not *the* person. My team can be nurtured to grow and do more. I am not so important."

For a lawyer who'd built everything on being the important one, that's a massive emotional shift.

The Conversations No One Wants to Have

Lin McCraw took a family-owned law firm in a smallish Texas town, quit practicing door law to focus on Personal Injury, and, over the past 10 years, has grown the firm to over $14 million in annual revenue. He's done EOS. He's built teams. And he'll tell you something most people don't want to hear: "You will lose people if you do EOS. You've got to be comfortable with that. And it will happen at high levels."

This makes lawyers incredibly nervous. We like to think of our teams as family. We've known these people for years. We can't just let them go, right?

"I recommend that you don't call your people family," Lin said. "They're teammates."

Wait, what?

"With family, you've got to put up with all kinds of crap. You're stuck with them. That brother-in-law is still your brother-in-law, no matter what he said or did.

Teammates are something different. We perform for each other. We create a cohesive whole that's better than the sum of the parts."

This isn't cold. It's honest. A high-performing team requires everyone pulling their weight in the right direction. Family obligations mean accepting dysfunction. Team excellence means addressing it.

When you complete The People Analyzer, you're going to discover uncomfortable truths. That person you've been making excuses for? They don't fit your values, or they're not good at their job, or both. That Terrorist who brings in revenue but makes everyone miserable? They need to go or genuinely change.

> **A high-performing team requires everyone pulling their weight in the right direction.**

The conversations are hard. Have them anyway. Here are some sample phrases to use in these situations:

For Right Person, Wrong Seat: "We value you here, and you fit our culture. This seat isn't working. Let's find you a seat where you can be a Star."

For Wrong Person, Right Seat: "You're productive, but you don't fit our culture. Here's what needs to change. Let's meet again in 30 days, and if the behavior hasn't improved, we'll count that as a strike. If you get to three strikes, we'll help you find a better fit elsewhere."

For Wrong Person, Wrong Seat: Follow the same 3-Strike Process for this person. If they reach three strikes, say, "This isn't working for either of us. Let's make a plan to transition you out with dignity."

These conversations feel terrible in the moment. But six months later, when your firm is humming and your remaining team members are thriving? You'll wish you'd done it sooner.

And don't forget...

Right Person, Right Seat: Your Stars want and need your attention. Give them your love, tell them how awesome they are, how much you appreciate them, and ask if there is anything you can do to help them.

How to Get It Done

Can you implement EOS on your own? Sure. Many firms do it successfully. You read the books, work through the tools, build your Accountability Chart, complete your People Analyzers, and make the hard decisions.

The question is: will you?

Here's what typically goes wrong with self-implementation. You cherry-pick the tools you like and skip the uncomfortable ones. You build seats around your existing people instead of defining what your firm truly needs. You complete The People Analyzer, and then do nothing about what it reveals. You start cutting Level 10 Meetings short to avoid the issues portion because those conversations are hard. You let problems slide because, well, you're busy, and surely this can wait until next quarter.

Who's going to call you on it?

A Professional EOS Implementer sees what you can't see. Maybe you're too close to someone who's been with you for years. Perhaps you're intimidated by your rainmaker. Maybe you're making excuses for someone because they "really need this job." An Implementer spots these patterns immediately and helps you get honest about reality.

They facilitate the uncomfortable conversations. They hold you accountable for the decisions you keep postponing. They help you move faster because they've done this hundreds of times and know what works. They have no dog in the fight except getting you to the Right People in the Right Seats.

Generally, the firms that succeed fastest with the People Component® have outside help. Not because they're not smart enough to do it themselves, but because having someone who's not emotionally invested makes the hard decisions easier.

The Relief You Didn't Know You Needed

Here's what Lynn said about her EOS journey that I think captures something profound:

"It feels to me like it gives me more legitimacy to call myself a business owner. Not so much masquerading as a lawyer-turned-entrepreneur. I am a business owner."

That identity shift matters more than you might think. When you're trapped in the lawyer mindset, you believe everything depends on you. When you step into the business owner mindset, you build systems and teams that can run without you.

Lynn's team has been with her for more than five years. They're loyal, capable, good people. But they needed structure. They needed clear seats with clear responsibilities. They needed a leader (Randie) who could help them grow.

And Lynn needed to not be *the* person anymore.

"That Accountability Chart's awfully good," she said. "Just put me in the Visionary seat."

That's the thing about the People Component that most lawyers don't realize: it's not just about evaluating your team. It's about giving yourself permission to step out of roles that are killing you.

Right People in Right Seats isn't a theory. It's not an aspirational goal. It's the daily reality of firms that really work.

You now know how to assess your people honestly. You know what seats you need. You know the conversations you've been avoiding.

The question is: what are you going to do about it?

In the next chapter, we'll tackle what happens once you have the right team: How do you know if they're truly performing? How do you make decisions based on reality instead of hope?

It's time to talk about data. The kind that genuinely matters.

THE PEOPLE ANALYZER®

NAME

THE BAR

| RATING: + +/- - | NUMBER OF + : _______ | NUMBER OF +/- : _______ | Y | Y | Y |

Chapter Eight

Why Successful Firms Run on Numbers, Not Gut Feel

You built the right team in Chapter 7. Now comes the question every law firm owner dreads: How do you know if it's truly working?

The Dangerous Illusion of "Feeling Successful"

I've seen this happen in firm after firm. Revenue is up 40 percent, but the owner is taking home less money. It was the busiest year ever, yet the worst profit margins in history. "Best month" is immediately followed by "We can't make payroll." Sound familiar?

Mike Smith lived this nightmare. He has an estate planning practice in Savannah. It was growing like crazy, and he was working harder than ever, but personally making less money than the year before. "I remember sitting there thinking: How can the numbers look this good, and I still feel broke?" he told me.

The problem wasn't effort. Mike is brilliant, his team was solid, and clients loved the firm. The problem was that he was flying blind. He knew revenue, sure. He tracked billable hours, absolutely. But profit per plan? Cost per case? Cash flow forecasting? Those might as well have been written in hieroglyphics.

That's the gut feel trap that kills law firms. Revenue growth creates the illusion you're winning, but you never notice profit margins shrinking. Busy-ness confuses you into thinking activity equals productivity. The phones are ringing, the staff looks busy, so everything must be fine. Until the dreaded cash flow surprise comes: "We had our best month ever, so why can't I pay the bills?"

Mike lived that cycle for years. Revenue swinging 40–60 percent month to month, hiring more people when things looked good, then panicking when collections dropped. Investment paralysis because he couldn't make growth decisions without wondering if they'd bankrupt him. "I was successful on paper and broke in reality," he admitted.

Here's why lawyers resist data beyond billable hours: complexity avoidance ("Numbers are for accountants"), time pressure ("I don't have time to analyze reports"), and frankly, fear of bad news. Sometimes ignorance feels better than knowing you're not as profitable as you thought you were or want to be.

But the cost of flying blind is devastating. You miss profitable growth opportunities because you can't tell which practice areas or case types genuinely make money. You waste resources investing in the wrong areas. Stress amplifies because you're constantly worried about financial stability. And your team feels the uncertainty, which affects morale and retention.

The breakthrough for Mike came when he stopped focusing solely on revenue and began examining real numbers: profit, collections, and cost per case. "It was like someone turned the lights on," he recalled. "We went from flying blind to actually knowing where the money was going. And once I knew, I could finally make decisions with confidence."

When you know your numbers, you sleep better. When you understand your trends, you make better decisions. When you have predictable systems, you can honestly plan for growth instead of just hoping it happens.

Why Financial Systems Are My Secret Weapon

Most other books will tell you to track a few basic metrics, revenue, cost of goods sold (COGS), profit, accounts receivable (AR), and call it a day. They focus on generic business metrics because they're written for widget manufacturers and software companies, but don't address law firm financial complexity, things like realization rates, case cost allocation, or the cash flow nightmares of contingency practices. That's useful, but it's surface-level and doesn't address law firm-specific needs. They give you theory without law firm-specific implementation, missing the intricacy that makes or breaks law firms.

My background is different. MBA in Finance. CFA designation. And through Cathcap, I've served as a fractional CFO for hundreds of law firms. I've been inside the numbers, the real numbers, not just the pretty ones partners like to talk about. I've seen which firms make money versus which ones just look busy. EOS knows that Data needs to be fully integrated into your company. I know what Data you need to be integrating.

When you combine EOS people systems with sophisticated financial and data systems, you get predictable results.

When you combine EOS people systems with sophisticated financial and data systems, something magical happens. You don't just get better results; you get predictable results you can take to the bank. Literally.

Mike experienced this firsthand. Before EOS, he tracked billable hours and top-line revenue, but nothing deeper. He didn't realize his flat-fee model required different metrics than a traditional hourly shop. "I knew we were busy, but I didn't really know if we were making money on each plan," he admitted.

When we built out his financial dashboard, integrating EOS Scorecard measurables with cost-per-plan analysis, collections tracking, and margin calculations, he finally understood which plan types were profitable and which weren't. That clarity gave him confidence to hire, knowing the payroll would be covered. He could invest in marketing without fear of a cash crunch. He could price services based on their actual value rather than guessing.

But we couldn't get any of this information until we changed the way he did his books. Mike switched from a family friend who had been doing a great job reconciling his accounts and filing his taxes to Legal Ease Bookkeeping, a bookkeeping firm that works exclusively with law firms. Brandy Derrick, the owner, knew immediately what integrations needed to be done, how transactions needed to be categorized, and what tweaks had to be made so we could get the information we needed to make data-driven decisions.

Integrated Data + Finance looks like predictable profitability, where you know your profit before the month ends. Investment confidence to make data-driven growth decisions. Cash flow stability that eliminates financial surprises. And team accountability, where everyone understands their financial impact.

The EOS Scorecard: Your Firm's Vital Signs

A Scorecard isn't just a bunch of numbers on a spreadsheet. It's your firm's vital signs: 5 to 15 weekly activity-based measurables that predict future performance before problems explode. Think leading indicators that show trends before disasters appear, team alignment where everyone knows what success looks like, and a course correction tool that lets you make weekly adjustments instead of quarterly surprises.

Why does weekly matter more than monthly? Faster response time. Catch problems in week one, not week four. Team engagement stays high because people stay connected to results. You can identify trends developing early. And accountability becomes a rhythm with regular check-ins that create consistent performance.

But here's the part most firms miss: the 13 weeks of history sitting right there on your Scorecard. This isn't just this week's snapshot; it's three full months of patterns staring you in the face.

Mike discovered this when he noticed his consultation conversion rate dropping. Not just one bad week, three weeks in a row showing the same downward trend. "Without the 13-week view, I would have written off a bad week as just luck," he said. "But seeing it happen three times in a row? That's a pattern. That's a problem we need to solve."

The 13-week visual changed everything for his firm. They spotted seasonal patterns they'd never noticed before. Summer consultations always dropped, but fall plan completions always spiked. Armed with that knowledge, they adjusted marketing spend and staffing. They could prepare for slow periods rather than panic during them. They could hire before busy seasons, rather than scrambling when overwhelmed.

Let me show you some examples of what this can look like in the real world. To see the set-up, check out the diagram on page 96.

Personal Injury Firm Scorecard (like David and Rich's)
- New leads: Marketing effectiveness and pipeline health

- Consultation conversion rate: Sales process efficiency

- Cases signed: New matters acquired this week

- Cases closed: Matters resolved (settlements/verdicts)

- Average case value: Quality and pricing trends

- Cases in inventory: How much of your capacity are you using

- Cash collections: Actual money received

- Cases within parameters: Production efficiency and employee productivity

Estate Planning Firm Scorecard (like Mike and Lynn)
- Consultations scheduled: Lead generation effectiveness

- Plan completions: Productivity and throughput

- Average plan value: Pricing and service.level trends

- Client referrals: Satisfaction and growth indicator

- Days to completion: Efficiency and bottleneck identification

- Worked vs billed: How profitable was each matter vs the flat fee

Immigration Firm Scorecard (like Constance's)
- Clickthrough rate: Ad effectiveness

- Applications filed: Productivity and workflow efficiency

- Reject rates: Quality and success measurement

- Processing time per case type: Efficiency benchmarking

- Client communication score: Service quality indicator

- Revenue per case type: Profitability by service line

- Referral partner activity: Business development effectiveness

Here's the financial integration piece most firms miss: the measurables that drive profitability.

- Profit per partner/attorney: True productivity measurement

- Cost per case/matter: Actual profitability analysis

- Cash flow forecast accuracy: Predictability indicator

- Client acquisition cost: Marketing ROI measurement

- Lifetime client value: Long-term relationship profitability

Making numbers meaningful means setting a specific target for each measurable and using a green/yellow/red system for visual performance indicators. Track trends week-over-week and year-over-year. And always dig into the story behind the numbers. What drives performance up or down?

Mike's Scorecard transformation was dramatic. Before, he looked at revenue and hours. After, he tracked plan completions, average values, client referrals, and profit margins. "For the first time, I could see problems coming weeks before they hit," he said. "And I could see what was working so we could do more of it."

Financial Dashboards: Owner Confidence Through Clarity

Based on my experience, the owner's financial dashboard should give you everything you need to make confident decisions: current and projected 13-week cash flow; profitability trends showing margins by time period; a revenue pipeline with predictable future income streams; expense management with cost control and efficiency metrics; and growth investment ROI showing return on business development spending.

Here's a client story that shows the transformational power. Before implementing dashboards, this personal injury firm owner checked his bank balance daily and lived in constant worry. The problem? No visibility into financial trends or future performance. We implemented a custom dashboard showing key financial metrics. The first breakthrough came when the dashboard predicted a cash shortage six weeks before it would hit, giving him time to adjust. Long-term result? Increased profit margins while dramatically reducing owner stress.

Practice-specific financial insights make all the difference.

Contingency Firms need to track:

- Case investment tracking: Money invested versus potential return

- Settlement probability modeling: Expected value calculations

- Case cost allocation: True profitability by matter type

- Cash flow forecasting: Smoothing lumpy income through modeling

Hourly Billing Firms focus on:

- Collection rate analysis: Billed versus collected percentages

- Utilization tracking: Billable hours versus available hours

- Rate optimization: Pricing strategy based on demand and value

- Realization Rate analysis: Understanding and minimizing lost time: worked vs. billed

Flat Fee Firms monitor:

- Scope creep monitoring: Actual versus estimated time per matter

- Pricing model validation: Profitability by service type

- Capacity planning: Volume limits based on fixed pricing

- Value optimization: Premium pricing for specialized services

The confidence transformation is remarkable. You can make investment decisions based on data, not fear. You know exactly when you can afford new team members. You can charge what your services are actually worth. And you can plan growth based on facts, not hope.

Mike described it perfectly: "Before dashboards, I was always worried. After dashboards, I am always planning. That's the difference between running a practice and owning a business."

Weekly financial discipline makes it work. Monday morning ritual: review weekend dashboard updates. Share selected metrics with appropriate staff. Have weekly team conversations about performance. Make minor course corrections that prevent big problems.

Mike's team now starts every Monday by reviewing their dashboard together. Not a boring finance meeting; a quick 15-minute pulse check. Revenue tracking looks good. Collections on target. Any yellow flags to address? Then they move on to client work, confident they know exactly where they stand.

"We changed some things about our revenue model, and now I have the ability to track revenue and then what our collection is, revenue collected on a weekly basis," Mike explained. "And so that gives me a good indicator of where we are from a cash standpoint. That's been huge."

You can't do this without what is called continuous accounting. Continuous accounting means that your books are updated at least once a week. When interviewing bookkeepers, this is one of the most important questions to ask: "How often do you accept transactions and update my books?" Brandy at Legal Ease Bookkeeping says, "Bookkeeping should be done at least weekly. If you wait longer, the information starts losing its value. Transactions get fuzzy, details are forgotten, and answering simple questions turns into a research project. When the books are updated every week, the numbers stay meaningful, and clients can quickly answer questions about transactions while the details are still fresh." If your books aren't being updated on a regular basis, it will render your dashboard and your ability to predict worthless.

Building Predictable Profitability

Here's the difference between firms that grow and firms that scale: predictability. Growing firms get bigger and busier. Scaling firms get bigger and more profitable. The difference is in the systems. The predictability framework has four pillars: revenue forecasting with multiple models for different practice types; expense budgeting covering fixed and variable cost management; profit planning with target margins and achievement strategies; and cash flow modeling with 13-week rolling forecasts and scenario planning.

Let's break down revenue predictability by practice type because what works for personal injury won't work for estate planning.

Contingency Practice Revenue Model

The challenge here is lumpy income. You might go months with minimal collections, then hit three settlements in one week. Predictability seems impossible, right? Wrong.

Track these five drivers:

- Case acquisition rates: New matters per month by source

- Settlement timing patterns: Historical data on case resolution

- Average case values: By case type and complexity

- Success rate factors: Win rates by attorney and case type

- Collection timing: When settlements convert to cash

One personal injury firm I worked with had been operating for 15 years but had never analyzed their settlement patterns. When we pulled the data, we discovered settlements spiked in November and March like clockwork, and insurance companies clear cases before the fiscal year-ends. Armed with that knowledge, they could predict cash flow six months out and plan accordingly. While they can't change lumpy income, they plan for it and ensure they don't have a lumpy *supply* of cash.

Subscription/Retainer Model

This is the holy grail of predictability, but only if you track the right metrics:

- Monthly recurring revenue: Predictable base income

- Client retention rates: How long clients typically stay

- Upsell opportunities: Additional services to existing clients

- Capacity planning: Maximum clients per attorney or staff level

- Pricing optimization: Rate increases and client response

Mike's estate planning practice doesn't quite fit the subscription model, but he's built predictability through his flat-fee structure. He knows exactly how many consultations turn into plans, how long each plan takes to complete, and what his margins are. That predictability lets him forecast revenue three months out with 90 percent accuracy.

Project-Based Model

Business law, transactional work, and complex litigation are where most firms live. Predictability requires tracking:

- Pipeline conversion rates: Proposals to signed agreements

- Project duration patterns: How long matters truly take to complete

- Scope change frequency: Additional work beyond what was originally anticipated

- Seasonal variations: Busy and slow periods by practice area

- Referral source reliability: Predictable work from key sources

Expense predictability and control are the other side of the equation. You can't control what you can't measure.

Fixed cost management covers rent, insurance, technology, and core staff. These don't change month to month, which makes them easy to predict but hard to optimize. Variable cost tracking matters more: costs that scale with revenue or activity. When you know your variable cost ratio (how much each dollar of revenue costs to generate), you can model profitability at different revenue levels.

Investment timing becomes strategic instead of reactive. When should you hire? Maybe when your revenue trend supports the additional payroll for six months, not just this month. When should you expand? Potentially when your capacity utilization hits 85 percent consistently for a quarter. When should you upgrade systems? Usually, when the time savings pay back your investment within 18 months.

Efficiency improvements through technology and process investments need ROI analysis. Don't buy software because it's cool. Buy it because the time savings, when multiplied by your hourly rate, exceed the cost within a certain time frame.

Mike's transformation from erratic to predictable took twelve months. Starting point: Revenue swings of 40–60 percent month to month. We identified the business drivers he'd never tracked. Implemented revenue forecasting and expense budgeting. Monthly improvements showed variance decreasing steadily. Final result: Revenue predictable within 10 percent, profit margins stable. Owner transformation: From stress to confidence, fear to planning.

The compound effect of predictability changes everything. Better decision-making because you can evaluate opportunities rationally. Stress reduction because you know what's coming financially. Team stability with consistent employment and growth opportunities. Clients benefit because a stable firm provides better service. And growth because a predictable base income enables expansion planning.

"I've now gotten to a point where I kind of think the sky's the limit in terms of how much we can grow," Mike said. "And that doesn't mean that there aren't problems that need to be solved. But I look at things now as, well, that's a business problem, and we need to address the issue and figure out how to solve the issue."

That's the mindset shift predictability creates. From victim to problem-solver. From reactive to strategic. From stressed to confident.

You Don't Have to Do This Alone

If you've made it this far in the chapter, you might be feeling a little overwhelmed. Revenue forecasting models. Cash flow modeling. Realization rates, utilization tracking, and profitability analysis by practice area.

Take a breath. I'm not expecting you to become an accountant or financial analyst.

You're an attorney. You went to law school, not business school. Nobody taught you how to build a financial dashboard or analyze profit margins by matter type. You learned contracts and torts and civil procedure. Running a high-level financial operation? That wasn't on the bar exam.

And that's not your fault. It's just reality.

I learned this firsthand years ago when I was running the finances for my family's boutique corporate litigation firm. A consultant we'd hired for sales and marketing started sending his other clients my way. They wanted to know if I could do for them what I was doing for my family. That's when I discovered something that genuinely surprised me: successful attorneys running established firms who had no idea what their numbers really meant. They were making million-dollar decisions based on gut instinct because they didn't have the tools or training to do anything else.

It wasn't that they were bad at business. They'd never been taught to run one. Law school prepared them to practice law, not to analyze cash flow cycles or build profit forecasts.

That realization led me to found Cathcap almost fifteen years ago. We've worked with hundreds of law firms since then, providing fractional CFO services. The concept is simple: instead of hiring a full-time CFO at $250,000 or more annually, you bring in financial expertise on a part-time basis. You get strategic thinking at a fraction of the cost.

The good news is that there are plenty of companies out there offering fractional CFO services. The model has grown significantly over the past decade, and you have options. But here's what I'd encourage you to look for.

First, find someone who specializes in law firms. Your finances are weird. Trust accounting, contingency fee timing, the way cases move through your pipeline... none of that works like a normal business. Generic financial consultants spend half their time just trying to understand your model. You want someone who already speaks your language.

Second, watch out for the experience mismatch. Firms often hire someone full-time who's too junior to provide real strategy, or they bring in someone senior who thinks detailed analysis is "beneath them." They want to talk high-level but won't dive deep into the data. Strategy without substance is just guessing in a nicer suit.

At Cathcap, every CFO has an analyst working alongside them. The CFO brings strategic thinking and leadership team presence. The analyst digs into your data, builds the models, and surfaces insights that make the strategy truly insightful and effective. You get high-level guidance backed by granular analysis. Whatever firm you choose, make sure you're getting both.

Full disclosure: I'm Cathcap's founder, though it's now run by our Integrator. I mention it because I've spent fifteen years watching attorneys struggle with finances they were never trained to manage. You don't have to become a numbers person. You just have to be smart enough to get help from people who truly know this stuff.

Your job is to be the attorney. Let someone else be the CFO.

By the way, all of these things hold true for bookkeepers as well. You should never ever do your own books. If your billable rate is $350-500 an hour, why would you spend that time doing bookkeeping? That time is much better spent practicing law. Second, find one who specializes in law firms. You shouldn't pay for their learning curve. And last, that bargain "CFO" that's willing to come in-house? They are a bookkeeper looking for a raise who knows nothing about the legal industry. It's why, at Cathcap, we almost always suggest working with a service like Legal Ease Bookkeeping instead of trying to bring it in-house before you hit eight figures.

Individual Measurables: Cascading Accountability

EOS takes the Scorecard concept and makes it personal. It's not enough to have firm-wide measurables that only the owner cares about. You need every single person in your firm to be accountable for their own numbers.

This is the measurables cascade. It starts with your leadership team Scorecard. Then each department builds their own Scorecard. Finally, each individual owns one, two, or three specific numbers. Not vague goals like "work hard" or "provide good service." Activity-based numbers they can track weekly.

Think about that for a second. Every person in your firm, from the senior partner to the receptionist, looks at their own Scorecard every week, knowing exactly whether they're hitting their targets or falling short. No more subjective performance discussions. No more "I think I'm doing well" based on gut feel, just numbers, trends, and accountability.

Mike's estate planning paralegal owns client satisfaction scores. Every time she talks to a client, she asks a couple of questions from their survey and records the responses. "We created a system where our estate planning paralegal slips in a couple of questions from our survey form every time she talks to a client and puts that data into the form," Mike explained. "She has to interpret what their response is, what kind of score we get. But that's giving us the ability to have some insight into whether we're really pleasing the clients like we think we are."

The paralegal doesn't wait for annual reviews to find out if she's doing well. She knows every single week. Her Scorecard shows client satisfaction trending up or down. If it drops, she can investigate immediately. If it's climbing, she knows her method is working.

Mike's intake coordinator owns consultation conversion rates. How many people who schedule consultations actually show up? Of those who show, how many become clients? Those are her numbers. She tracks them weekly. When conversion drops, she digs into why. Were the leads of lower quality? Did something change in the scheduling process? Is there a new competitor in town?

"One of our measurables is task completion percentage," Mike said. "And we use Clio to handle our case management. Tasks are assigned to various roles based on where we are in a matter. And one of the things that we always had trouble with was really knowing whether everything was under control. And now we're tracking week by week, how many tasks are complete. Our goal for that is 100 percent because then we know that everything's on track."

When task completion dropped dramatically one week, Mike didn't have to wonder if there was a problem. The Scorecard screamed it at him. "We saw a big dip in that last week, as a matter of fact. And that sent me to go find out what was going on. That led to some uncomfortable conversations."

But here's the beautiful part: those uncomfortable conversations were based on objective data, not subjective feelings. Mike wasn't accusing anyone of being lazy or not caring. He was looking at a number that dropped and asking what systemic problem caused it. It turned out they'd implemented a new workflow that created bottlenecks. They fixed the workflow, and task completion bounced back.

The uncomfortable conversations are based on objective data, not subjective feelings.

This is accountability without micromanagement. Clear expectations where everyone knows their numbers and targets. Self-monitoring, where team members track their own performance. Peer accountability, where team members help each other succeed. And a coaching approach that uses data to help people improve, not punish them for missing goals.

Remember those right people in the right seats from Chapter 7? Now you have the tools to measure if they're performing. Remember that compelling vision from Chapter 6? Now everyone knows if their daily work is moving the firm toward it.

Mike put it perfectly: "The numbers gave me freedom. I didn't have to hover anymore. I could see if someone was on track, and so could they. The accountability became part of the culture instead of something I had to enforce."

Data-Driven Team Performance

Individual measurables create personal accountability. Team performance metrics create collective responsibility. Both matter.

Individual performance metrics should measure what matters for each seat. Attorney productivity gets tracked through revenue per hour, matters handled, and client satisfaction scores. Support staff efficiency shows up in tasks completed, error rates, and client feedback. Business development activities include acquiring new clients, generating referrals, and building relationships. And financial contribution reveals the direct profit impact of each team member.

But law firms don't succeed through individual heroics. They win through teamwork. That's where team performance integration comes in.

Department Scorecards create group measurables that drive collaboration. The litigation team doesn't just track individual attorney billings; they track total department profitability, case win rates, and client retention. When those numbers dip, the whole team rallies to fix them.

Cross-functional goals require teamwork to achieve. Client experience scores become shared responsibility between attorneys and staff. One firm I worked with made "client referral rate" a shared metric across their entire team. Suddenly, everyone from the receptionist to the senior partner was thinking about how to earn referrals. The measurable went from 15 percent of new business from referrals to 45 percent in 18 months.

Profitability targets ensure everyone understands their financial impact. Mike's team knows their target profit margin per plan. They see what scope creep costs. They know which services generate the best margins. When someone suggests taking on work that doesn't fit their profitable model, the whole team pushes back. Not because they're being difficult, but because they understand the financial impact.

Performance review transformation happens naturally when you have objective data. Subjective evaluations (you seem to be working hard; I think clients like you) are replaced by measurable facts (your client satisfaction score is 9.2, up from 8.7 last quarter). Regular feedback happens weekly in team meetings, rather than once-a-year reviews that nobody likes. Development planning focuses on specific metric improvement goals (let's get your consultation conversion rate from 40 percent to 50 percent). And compensation alignment ties pay to measurable value creation.

One associate at Mike's firm was frustrated that she wasn't getting paid what she thought she deserved. Fair concern. So Mike showed her the numbers. Her plan completion rate was 20 percent below the firm's average. Her client satisfaction scores were solid but not exceptional. Her referral generation was basically zero.

"Here's the deal," Mike told her. "Get your completion rate to firm average, maintain your satisfaction scores, and generate three client referrals per quarter. Do that for six months, and we'll talk compensation."

No argument. No hurt feelings. Just clear expectations and a path forward. Six months later, she'd hit every target. Mike gave her the raise. She earned it, and the numbers proved it.

Technology Integration: Making Data Easy

Let's be honest: lawyers don't go into the profession for their love of tech. Most would rather draft a 40-page brief than set up a new dashboard. But if you want your firm to run on data instead of gut feel, you need the right technology stack. The good news? It doesn't have to be complicated.

The essential technology stack starts with your practice management system, which serves as the central hub for case and client data. Clio, Filevine, CASEpeer, whatever you use, this needs to be the single source of truth for everything client-related. Your financial management system should integrate directly with operations, so billing and collections aren't a separate universe: QuickBooks, Xero, or even a more sophisticated system like NetSuite for larger firms. Dashboard tools pull data into clean, easy-to-understand visual reports. Try Strety, Domo, or Power BI. There are tons of options. And time tracking captures accurate data for analysis, whether you bill hourly or not.

Integration challenges are real. Most firms suffer from data silos where systems don't talk to each other. Your practice management system knows about cases. Your accounting system knows about money. And your CRM knows about your marketing activities. But they don't share information, so you have to reconcile everything manually. Manual reporting wastes time and creates delayed information that's weeks behind reality. And user adoption remains the biggest hurdle. Getting attorneys and staff to consistently use systems can feel like herding cats.

Mike ran into every one of these issues. "We had systems, but they weren't connected," he admitted. "I was paying for reports that took forever to compile and were already outdated when I got them. It felt like we were always behind."

The breakthrough came when Mike invested in integration. Not fancy, just smart. His practice management system now feeds data directly into his financial dashboard. Client acquisition costs are automatically generated by marketing software. Task completion percentages are pulled from his case management system in real-time. No more manual updates. No more stale data.

"I use High Level for marketing and lead tracking," Mike explained. "It's a custom version, and we use Consolidated for dashboards. It's not perfect. Because it's not built into one system, there's always some friction. But it's infinitely better than what we had before."

Implementation best practices start simple: begin with 3–5 key metrics. Don't try to track everything on day one. Pick the numbers that matter most and get those dialed in. Automate data collection to minimize manual entry requirements. If someone has to update the dashboard by hand, it won't happen as consistently. Hold regular weekly reviews where the team discusses numbers. Make it part of your rhythm. And continuously improve by adding metrics as the system matures.

ROI measurement shows the value. Time savings reduce administrative overhead. Mike used to spend four hours a month compiling reports. Now his dashboard updates automatically, and he spends 30 minutes reviewing it. Faster decision-making comes from working with current data rather than stale reports. Error reduction improves because numbers come directly from the source rather than being transcribed multiple times. And growth enablement means systems support expansion without complexity explosion.

"The software is good, but every now and then things don't work perfectly," Mike admitted. "Sometimes the dashboard doesn't load when you want it to. But you know what? Even when it's frustrating, it's still better than flying blind. Once the data was flowing automatically, we could finally focus on growth instead of chasing numbers."

Technology doesn't run your firm for you, but it makes running on data simple, fast, and, dare I say, almost painless.

Numbers Show Problems, They Don't Solve Them

At this point, you've built the data foundation. You can clearly see your firm, track performance week to week, and predict profitability with confidence. For the first time, you're not relying on gut feel or panicked glances at the bank balance.

But here's the thing: problems are still going to happen. Equipment breaks. Staff quits. Clients complain. Cases go sideways. The difference is in how you handle them.

Most law firms see a problem and react. Yellow flag on the Scorecard? Panic. Trend going the wrong direction? The owner swoops in to save the day. Again.

EOS firms respond systematically. Yellow flag? Put it on the Issues list for the next L10 to Identify, Discuss, and Solve (IDS®) to resolve it. Trend dropping? Root cause analysis to fix it permanently. Issue pops up? Team solves it together.

Your data dashboard is flashing yellow on client satisfaction. Your Scorecard shows consultation conversion dropping three weeks in a row. Your cash flow forecast predicts a shortage in six weeks. Now what?

EOS firms respond systematically.

Remember Mike's task completion percentage dropping? The Scorecard showed the problem. But the team had to dig into why, discover the workflow bottleneck, fix the process, and verify the solution worked. That's the Issues Component® of EOS.

Data gives you visibility to see problems coming. But seeing them isn't enough. You need a systematic way to solve them permanently. Not band-aid fixes that last a week. Not owner heroics that burn you out. Real solutions that make problems go away forever.

In the next chapter, I'll show you exactly how to transform your firm from firefighting mode to problem-solving machine.

COMPANY SCORECARD

3/29											
3/22											
3/15											
3/8											
3/1											
2/23											
2/16											
2/9											
2/2											
1/26											
1/19											
1/12											
1/5											
GOAL											
MEASURABLES											
WHO											

Chapter Nine

How Successful Firms Solve Problems For Good

B y the time you've built your dashboards and your scorecard, you finally have the visibility you always wanted. You can see the numbers. You can see the patterns. And then... one of those patterns dips. A metric turns yellow. Something looks off.

Most law firms respond by tightening their grip and managing the problem. But great firms don't manage problems; they solve them.

Why Law Firms Are Stuck in Firefighting Mode

Unfortunately, most lawyers live in firefighting mode without ever realizing they're doing it.

Not the dramatic firefighting people imagine, angry clients storming the office, blown deadlines, or malpractice-level chaos. Mike Griffin and Chuck Welsh of ACCEL Law Group, a transactional M&A firm in West Hartford, Connecticut, weren't dealing with anything like that. Their firm wasn't crumbling. Their work was of high quality. Their clients were happy. And they had grown ACCEL Law Group much faster than they originally anticipated.

They were successful. Profitable. Growing steadily.

And completely stuck.

When Mike described their pre-EOS operations to me, he didn't talk about disasters. He talked about mornings when he'd sit down at his desk, and somehow a small line of people would form outside his door. He described it as a "deli line." A paralegal needing clarity on a matter. An associate needing a decision. Someone on the ops side needing direction before they could move forward.

None of it was urgent enough to be dramatic. But all of it was important enough to stop someone in their tracks.

These weren't "fires." They were friction points, small, constant, recurring challenges that made everyone dependent on the partners to move work forward. Mike and Chuck weren't running a chaotic firm. They were running a highly functional firm that had reached the natural limit of what two human beings can answer in a day.

As Mike put it: "To maintain our positive trajectory, Chuck and I had to work harder and harder. We grew the law firm to 10 attorneys and were closing 40-plus transactions each year, but the firm was still too reliant on the two of us, and we were not leveraging the deeper bench. This led to budgets being missed and frustration between the founders and our team. We had no 'operating system' or shared vision."

Think about that for a second. They weren't failing. They were succeeding themselves into a corner.

They had done what most law firm owners dream of: built a profitable practice, hired good people, and grown their client base. But they'd hit the ceiling. The firm couldn't grow beyond what Mike and Chuck could personally manage because every decision, every question, every clarification funneled through them. And they had hit the point where they just couldn't work any harder.

They were also committed to perpetuation and creating a sustainable firm that didn't rely on the two of them for success. But how do you build that when you're the answer to every question?

And because they're smart, capable lawyers, they did what every smart, capable lawyer does when faced with a problem: they solved it. Right there on the spot. Every time. For everyone.

Which is exactly how firefighting begins.

It doesn't start with emergencies. It starts with repetition. It starts with déjà vu. It starts with that subtle, nagging sense of, "Why does this keep coming up?"

What made them stuck wasn't incompetence. It was dependency.

Their team wasn't coming to them because they were helpless. Their team came to them because nothing in the firm clearly said, "Here's how we solve this. Here's who decides this. Here's the process."

So every question funneled upward. Every decision bottlenecked. Every week, the same issues reappeared, wearing slightly different clothing. And every time, Mike or Chuck handled it, because handling things is what lawyers are trained to do.

That's the real trap. Law school teaches attorneys to react quickly, solve problems personally, and treat every issue like a case that demands a custom solution. So we do exactly that inside our firms. Over and over. Forever.

But internal issues aren't cases. They don't go away just because you resolved that one version of them. They come back until you solve the root cause.

Before EOS, Mike told me, "We were dealing with the same problems over and over. Nothing actually got solved." And that is the most common firefighting pattern I see in firms, not chaos, just a quiet, persistent quagmire.

They weren't falling behind. They just weren't moving forward.

And for most firms, the cost of that stall is enormous: Hours of partner time drained by questions that shouldn't require a partner. A team that starts to doubt whether anything will ever get "fixed." Momentum that evaporates every time someone stops to ask what to do next. A ceiling on growth that sits directly on top of the owners' bandwidth.

The turning point, the moment where firefighting finally stops, begins with one deceptively simple mindset shift:

Stop asking, **"How do I handle this?"** Start asking, **"How do I make sure this never happens again?"**

That was the moment things finally changed for Mike and Chuck. And it's where we turn next.

The EOS Issues System: From Managing to Solving

Here's the fundamental mindset shift that changed everything for Chuck and Mike. Instead of repeatedly putting out the same fires, you install sprinkler systems.

From reactive to proactive: Chuck would spot problems and get frustrated, but they'd treat each incident as a unique crisis. With EOS, they learned to prevent issues instead of just responding to them.

From individual to systematic: Mike used to handle everything personally. The new approach meant creating processes instead of relying on heroic interventions.

From symptoms to root causes: Before EOS, they'd put Band-Aids on problems. Afterward, they learned to permanently fix the underlying problems.

From fire chief to fire prevention: Mike's role transformed from time-challenged problem-solver to the person who designs problem-prevention systems.

The good news about all those issues piling up in your firm is that there are only about 23 issues in the history of business. Seriously. Every problem you face? Someone else has already dealt with it. The key is getting really good at solving issues as they arise, solving them at the root, and making them go away for the long-term greater good of your firm.

> **There are only about 23 issues in the history of business.**

The Issues Component uses two tools and disciplines to help you do exactly that.

The Issues List: Your Problem Inventory

The Issues List becomes your firm's comprehensive problem inventory. Every issue, every headache, every "why does this keep happening?" moment gets captured. Nothing is too small. Nothing gets forgotten. Problems don't slip through cracks because there's a system to catch them all.

What makes the Issues List powerful is that it's about migrating a discipline and a culture down into your organization. You're creating an environment where everybody feels absolutely comfortable raising their hand, acknowledging problems, and calling them out. You're building a place where people say, "We've got an Issue," so that all your Issues get on a list somewhere throughout the organization.

For Chuck and Mike, this meant everything from client and team communication problems and budget issues to workflow bottlenecks finally had a home. No more hoping someone would remember. No more assuming it would fix itself. If it was a problem, it went on the list.

The Issues List doesn't solve these problems. It just makes sure you truly see them, capture them, and prioritize them. That's where the second tool comes in.

IDS: The Issue Solving Track

Even great teams struggle to really solve their Issues at the root. Very specifically, great leadership teams get themselves in a room, tackle an Issue, and end up discussing the shit out of it. Rarely do they come close to identifying the real root cause of the Issue. Rarely do they ever walk out having agreed on a plan of attack that will make the Issue go away forever. Rarely do they solve anything.

That's why EOS created the Issue Solving Track, IDS for short. It simply stands for Identify, Discuss, and Solve. Three steps that keep you on track when solving Issues.

Identify: Dig Deep to Find the Real Problem

"I" requires you to dig beyond what's written on your Issues List. Many times, what's on the list is just a symptom. You have to dig, dig, dig, dig down into the firm to identify the real root cause. If you are stuck, look at the EOS Model; your answer will lie in one of the 6 Key Components.

"Clients are always mad" isn't an issue you can fix. That's a symptom. "Clients don't receive systematic status updates about their cases" is a process issue you can solve.

Chuck and Mike had "Cases taking too long to complete" on their Issues List. That's what they could see: deals dragging, timelines slipping, worrying about clients getting antsy. When they dug deeper, they identified the real root cause: Work was literally stuck waiting on them. As Chuck put it: "Mike and I were the blockers." Files sat on their desks. Decisions waited for their approval. Strategic direction required their input. The team had the capacity and capability to move work forward, but everything bottlenecked at the two partners.

Discuss: Brief and Focused

Once you've identified the real root cause, discuss the Issue briefly with no one repeating themselves. Here's the rule that changed everything for Chuck and Mike: Saying it more than once is politicking.

You share your perspective, your concerns, your ideas. Then you're done. You don't repeat yourself. You don't grandstand. You don't try to win people over through endless discussion. This is super hard for attorneys. And just because you rephrased it doesn't mean it's a new idea. Once you've said your piece, you move on.

In Chuck and Mike's case, the discussion was short: Why was work waiting on them? Because no one else had clear authority to make decisions. The team wasn't incompetent; they were unclear. They didn't know which decisions they could make independently and which ones required partner review. So they played it safe and waited. Every time. For everything. The problem was structural, not personal.

Solve: Make It Go Away Forever

When people run out of ideas, you move to Solve. You work together to agree on a plan of attack that will make the Issue go away forever. That typically requires a decision, and somebody has to agree to take action to make the Issue go away forever.

Notice that language: "go away forever." Not "manage better this week." Not "handle if it comes up again." Forever.

For Chuck and Mike's bottleneck issue, the solution was systematic: Start with their Accountability Chart since everybody's roles and responsibilities were clearly outlined there. Make sure everybody understands their role and the parameters of their decision-making authority. Then start directing questions to the right person on the chart to get them answered.

The work started moving. Not because Mike and Chuck started working faster, but because they stopped being required for every decision. They eliminated the bottleneck by distributing authority appropriately.

Once that's done, you simply consider Issue #1 solved and move on to #2.

Eventually, you get to the point where your team is solving three, six, nine Issues per meeting, solving them at the root for the long-term greater good of the firm. Not managing them. Not discussing them endlessly. *Solving them.*

Why IDS Works for Legal Minds

IDS appeals to how lawyers already think. It's a logical progression that matches your analytical training. The thorough investigation is similar to legal research and discovery. Evidence-based conclusions mean facts drive decisions, not emotions. And permanent resolution? That's like establishing legal precedent; you handle it once, the right way, and it becomes the standard going forward.

Chuck discovered this: "I think the thing that I've taken away the most is this whole concept of solving issues. This is the issue. We articulated it. We got through it. This is who's going to take it. This is what's going to happen next. Okay, we solved that issue."

Common Mistakes in Issue Resolution

Chuck and Mike, like everybody, made almost every mistake in the book initially. Here are some to avoid:

- **Jumping to solutions:** Skipping the Identify and Discuss phases because you "already know" what to do. Spoiler: You don't. You know how to address the symptom, not the root cause.

- **Symptom focus:** Addressing effects versus causes. Training people to answer client calls better instead of creating a system that prevents unnecessary calls.

- **Individual blame:** Asking "Who did this?" instead of "How did this happen?" The first question creates defensiveness. The second creates solutions.

- **Incomplete follow-through:** Not ensuring solutions truly work. You make a decision, everyone feels good, then nobody verifies that the problem ever went away.

Issue Categories Specific to Law Firms

In firm after firm, I've seen the same five categories of problems show up repeatedly. You're not alone. Chuck and Mike dealt with a version of most of these. Watch how IDS transforms each type.

Client Experience Issues

Issues like "What's the status of my case?" calls that make you want to throw your phone out the window. Service delivery that's inconsistent, depending on who touched the file. Billing disputes that erupt because clients were surprised by fees they never saw coming.

Sound familiar?

IDS in Action

- **Issue:** Clients upset about surprise legal bills

- **Identify:** No upfront cost estimates or billing explanations (dig past "clients are angry" to find the real problem)

- **Discuss:** Finance team and attorneys agree, everyone assumed someone else was handling fee discussions

- **Solve:** Standardized cost estimation process plus monthly billing summaries with estimates for remaining work

- **Result:** Billing disputes virtually eliminated

Team Performance Issues

What looks like an attitude problem is often a training problem. Mike and Chuck discovered this the hard way. Role confusion meant Mike would assume Chuck was handling something, Chuck would assume Mike was handling it, and employees would wait for both to respond. Skills gaps created quality issues that required attorney rework. Communication breakdowns turned into information black holes.

IDS in Action

- **Issue:** Paralegal errors causing attorney rework (expensive and frustrating)

- **Identify:** Unclear quality standards and insufficient training (not incompetence, lack of clarity)

- **Discuss:** Paralegals admitted they were guessing at standards; attorneys realized they'd never documented expectations

- **Solve:** Detailed checklists, weekly quality reviews, plus targeted skills training

- **Result:** Error rates dropped dramatically, attorney time freed up for actual legal work

Operational Efficiency Issues

Process breakdowns create the workflow bottlenecks that make you crazy. Technology that doesn't talk to other technology means duplicate data entry and wasted hours. Uneven workloads where one attorney is drowning while others have capacity. Quality that varies wildly depending on who does the work.

IDS in Action

- **Issue:** Cases taking too long to close (hurting client satisfaction and cash flow)

- **Identify:** No standard process for case completion tasks (everyone invented their own approach)

- **Discuss:** The team discovered twelve different methods for closing files, and all were incomplete

- **Solve:** Case closing checklist plus clear responsible party assignments and deadline tracking

- **Result:** Cases closed 40 percent faster, clients happier, cash flow improved

Business Development Issues

You're working too hard for the clients you're getting. Marketing effectiveness suffers because you're not tracking what actually generates clients versus what just feels busy. Referral relationships deteriorate because you have no systematic way to maintain them. Networking becomes random coffee meetings with no follow-up system. Or my favorite, you've quit net*working* and started net*socializing*.

IDS in Action

- **Issue:** Declining referrals from a key source (a referral partner who used to send steady business)

- **Identify:** Lack of systematic relationship maintenance (out of sight, out of mind)

- **Discuss:** The team realized they only called referral sources when they needed something

- **Solve:** Monthly referral source contact schedule plus value-add communication plan (share relevant articles, invite to events, provide market updates)

- **Result:** Referrals from that source increased 60 percent within six months

Financial and Growth Issues

Examples of financial and growth Issues include:
- Cash flow problems from slow collections.

- Profitability challenges because you haven't reviewed pricing in three years.

- Growth obstacles where every expansion attempt requires more of your personal attention.

- Investment decisions about technology get delayed indefinitely because you're too busy firefighting to think strategically.

Chuck learned this lesson the expensive way: "You can't tackle everything in that 90-day period. It's okay to say, 'Yeah, we know this is an issue. We know this is a problem, but this isn't the focus for this quarter.'" Before IDS, they chased every issue like it was urgent. Bird, squirrel, shiny object, they were reactive to everything. IDS taught them to prioritize the three most important issues and solve them instead of spinning on twenty problems simultaneously.

Remember earlier when I said virtually every issue boiled down to either a people problem or a process problem? As you are digging for that root cause, simply ask yourself:

- Is this because the person involved is not a Core Values match (Right Person)

- Is this because the person doesn't GWC their seat (Right Seat)

- Is this because we don't know how to do it (no Process)

- Is this because the process is broken (fix it)

- Is this because the person didn't follow the process (more training)

These questions lead you to the root of the issue, making it significantly easier to find a long-term solution.

Every issue boils down to a people problem or a process problem.

Creating an Issues-Solving Culture

Moving from firefighting to systematic issue resolution requires cultural transformation. Chuck and Mike had to overcome natural lawyer resistance to this kind of systematic approach.

The cultural barriers they faced were real. Lawyers are trained to handle problems individually; each attorney is their own problem-solver. Admitting issues feels like admitting failure when your professional identity is built on having answers. Time constraints make systematic approaches feel impossible when you're already drowning. And confidentiality concerns create hesitation about openly discussing firm problems.

Mike describes the shift: "Initially, with just Chuck and me, we were keeping it pretty close to the vest, and in hindsight, that probably was not a good thing because we were trying to figure things out, address certain issues, and we weren't getting enough input."

Overcoming cultural resistance requires starting small: Begin with operational issues, not personality conflicts. Show ROI by demonstrating time saved and revenue protected. Create confidentiality protocols for discussing sensitive issues safely. Ensure leadership commitment, with partners visibly supporting the process.

The transformation happens when solving issues becomes how your firm operates, not something you do when you have time. When every team member knows they can raise an Issue and it will get addressed. When problems stop festering because there's a clear path to resolution.

Measuring Issue Resolution Success

How do you know if you're truly solving issues versus just managing them more efficiently? Chuck and Mike learned to track what matters.

Key metrics for issue resolution:

1. Issue closure rate measures the percentage of issues that are solved versus those that are simply managed.

2. Recurrence frequency tracks how often the same problems resurface.

3. Resolution time measures the average number of days from identification to solution.

4. Team satisfaction gauges confidence in the firm's problem-solving capability.

The transformation happened gradually. Mike explains: "Once we were nine months into this, we started to see the issues kind of crystallize. It's not a million issues up there. It's four issues. And maybe there are a lot of symptoms and maybe sub-issues, but we started to group them. That's where I feel like the traction comes from." Chuck quantified their transformation: "Process has been the biggest change... getting process, and thereby helping me get stuff off my plate, and then process in getting important decisions out there, getting people weighing in, and then getting past it, resolving it, whatever it might be."

You can also feel it when they've given up hope.

When issues pile up without follow-through, people stop bringing them up. When they are consistently solved, the entire culture shifts.

That's what happened in Mike and Chuck's firm. As soon as the team saw solutions being implemented, not talked about, not promised, but actually **rolled out and working**, their engagement spiked.

People started surfacing issues earlier.

They started asking bigger questions, not just the safe ones.

They started spotting opportunities, not just problems.

That is the mark of a healthy firm.

And you don't need a formal survey to measure that. You can see it in behavior long before it shows up in spreadsheets.

Tracking Systems:
How Firms Keep Issues From Disappearing

You don't need anything fancy to track issues. You can start with a simple shared document, though many firms eventually use their EOS software, practice management system, or a dedicated issues tool.

The core components stay the same:

- A living Issues List with status and ownership

- Meeting records that make decisions visible

- A follow-up calendar that ensures action actually happens

- A log of resolved issues so the team can see progress

Mike and Chuck saw immediate benefit here. Once issues were documented, everyone could literally *see* what needed attention and what fell through the cracks. Nothing lived in anyone's head anymore.

That alone can halve your stress.

The ROI of Issue Solving: What Firms Gain

Here's what firms experience when they track issue resolution effectively:

- **Time savings** from fewer disruptions and emergencies

- **Revenue protection** from preventing client confusion or dropped tasks

- **Team efficiency** from clearer expectations and fewer bottlenecks

- **Owner freedom** because problems are handled at the right level

Mike and Chuck didn't need a dramatic turnaround story. They needed clarity, the kind that lets strong leaders run an even stronger firm. And once they saw the ROI of systematically solving problems, the Issues List became not just a tool but a habit.

A habit that ratcheted up the trajectory of their business.

Technology Tools for Issue Management

One of the first things I tell firms when they start building an Issues List is this: the list only works if your team can actually *find* it. You'd be amazed at how many "systems" live on a legal pad under someone's lunch, buried in an inbox, or trapped inside whatever practice-management tool the firm bought three years ago but never learned to use. If your Issues List is wandering around the office like a stray dog, let's be honest, you don't have an Issues List. You have wishful thinking.

Technology won't magically solve your problems, but it *will* give your problem-solving system a stable home. The goal is simple: everyone needs one place to log issues, one place to review them, and one place to follow up. Whether that's a shared spreadsheet, a built-in feature of your practice-management software, or something more robust, the point is consistency. When the whole team knows exactly where issues live, the process becomes dramatically smoother. No more "Did someone write that down?" No more "Who's tracking this?" No more forgotten problems lurking in the shadows.

Once you have a home base for your issues, you also need a space where people can talk about them. That's where your Level 10 Meetings come in. Some teams meet around a physical table, others run L10s on Zoom, and some do it inside their EOS-specific software. The tool matters far less than the behavior it enables: a structured, reliable weekly pulse where issues aren't just acknowledged but truly solved. This is the moment when your Issues List becomes a living, breathing part of the business rather than something you look at once a quarter out of guilt.

The next piece is documentation, which represents the memory of your firm. A surprising number of teams solve an issue beautifully, celebrate, move on... aaaaaand then forget everything they just learned. Three months later, the same problem resurfaces, and the solution has to be reinvented all over again. Documentation prevents that. Whether it's stored in a shared drive, an intranet, or an internal knowledge base, every solved issue becomes part of the firm's institutional wisdom. Over time, your Issues List turns into a library of "here's how we fix this" instead of a recurring reminder of "here's what keeps going wrong."

You don't have to use dedicated EOS software. Plenty of firms run EOS successfully on spreadsheets and whiteboards. But for teams that want an easier way to track issues, collaborate between meetings, and link issues to Rocks, processes, and follow-through, purpose-built tools can feel like upgrading from a flip phone to a smartphone. They don't replace the work; they just make it smoother and more efficient.

Strety, my personal favorite, was built by people who run their business on EOS, which means it doesn't feel like software designed by someone who just read the book *Traction* once. It handles all your core EOS tools, L10s, Issues List, Rocks, Scorecards, Accountability Chart, in one place, and it plays nicely with whatever tech stack you're already using: Microsoft Teams, Google, Asana, your CRM, you name it. The interface is intuitive enough that your team will actually use it, which, let's be honest, is half the battle with any new software. And because issues, Rocks, and To Dos are all connected, you can see at a glance how everything relates. No more chasing information across five different platforms plus spreadsheets.

Of course, no technology in the world will help if your team doesn't use it. That's why the smartest firms start simple and build gradually. Pick one place to keep your Issues List. Pick one tool to support your L10s. Keep everything visible and easy to use. The goal isn't to build NASA's mission control; it's to build a system your paralegal, your associate, and your receptionist can all navigate confidently.

Mike and Chuck learned this almost immediately. Once their team knew exactly where to put issues, how they'd be discussed, and where decisions would be stored, everything changed. Conversations got clearer. Follow-through improved. And for the first time, they had a system that helped the whole team, not just the two of them, keep the firm running smoothly. Technology didn't solve their problems, but it did remove the friction that used to keep problems alive.

And that's the real purpose of tech in EOS: not complexity, not bells and whistles, not "corporate systems," but the simplest possible structure that genuinely gets used, every week, by every person, without drama.

By now, you can probably feel the shift happening inside Mike and Chuck's firm. Issues are no longer hiding in the shadows. Their team isn't whispering problems privately or leaving them on the partners' desks like unexploded grenades. Everything goes onto the Issues List. Everything gets addressed in the Level 10 Meeting. And everything gets solved, not with duct tape and hopeful thinking, but with real, permanent fixes.

But here's the part most firms don't see coming.

Once you start solving issues systematically, you begin to realize that *a lot* of your problems trace back to one root cause: no consistent way of doing the work in the first place. You start to fix a communication problem, only to discover the real cause was a missing process. You solve a recurring error in case files, and, surprise, the team has been improvising their own steps. You streamline a handoff between departments, and it becomes painfully clear that no one has ever documented how that handoff is supposed to work.

In other words, solving issues shines a harsh, helpful light on the fact that your firm has been running on habit, memory, and heroic effort, not systems. And while issue-solving is powerful, prevention is a whole different level of freedom.

This is exactly what happened once Mike and Chuck got good at IDS. They stopped firefighting, which was great. But then they realized: "Why are these fires starting at all?" Their breakthroughs, the ones that truly moved the firm forward, didn't come from solving issues. They came from installing the systems that made those issues impossible to begin with.

That's where we're headed next.

If Issues is about clearing the road in front of you, Process is about paving that road so it stays clear. Issues remove obstacles. Processes prevent them. Issues give you visibility. Processes give you consistency. Issues help you survive. Processes help you scale.

And let's be honest, you can't grow a healthy, profitable, independent law firm if every new case, every new client, and every new team member creates more chaos. At some point, you need the systems that deliver the same client experience, the same quality of work, and the same internal reliability, no matter who's doing the work.

So now that you've learned how to solve issues permanently, it's time to learn how to prevent them forever.

In the next chapter, we're going to build the processes that make your firm truly scalable, the same ones that finally gave Mike and Chuck the freedom to stop babysitting every detail and start leading their firm the way they always intended.

Chapter Ten

The Processes That Make Your Firm Scalable

You're solving issues systematically. Chuck and Mike proved that it works. But now let's take it to the next level: preventing those issues from happening in the first place.

The "Every Case Is Unique" Myth That Kills Growth

Every attorney tells me the same thing: "Brooke, you don't understand. Our work is too complex and unique to systematize. Every client situation is different. I can't turn my practice into a factory line."

I do understand. I've heard this exact objection from litigators, estate planners, PI attorneys, family law, immigration, intellectual property, and every other practice area you can name. And you know what? You're right. Every case does have its unique parts.

About 80 percent of legal work follow predictable patterns.

But here's the reality no one likes to admit: about 80 percent of legal work follows predictable patterns.

Think about that for a second. 80 percent. Not the complex legal strategy or the brilliant courtroom argument or the nuanced negotiation. That's the 20 percent that requires your expertise and judgment. But the intake process? The document requests? The client communication? The file management? The billing procedures? All predictable. All repeatable. All systematizable.

The belief that legal work is too unique to systematize is what kills growth in law firms. The cost of this thinking? Growth becomes limited by what the owner can personally oversee. You become the bottleneck. Every decision flows through you because nobody else knows "the right way" to do things. Because there is no documented right way.

And here's the irony that makes me laugh every time: Lawyers create processes for a living. You draft contracts, create operating agreements, and build systems for your clients. But when it comes to your own firm? Chaos with a billable hour attached.

Remember David Wolff and Rich Hall, partners at that Buffalo-based personal injury firm? Rich is the Visionary and has seen complete chaos at some firms, slightly more manageable chaos at others. David is the Integrator, brilliant at execution but drowning in the details of a rapidly growing practice.

Before they embraced systematic processes, their approach was close to pure chaos. David believed every client situation was too different to standardize. "Our work is too complex," he'd insist. The reality? Missed deadlines because there was no standard workflow. Inconsistent communication because everyone had their own "style." The quality varied dramatically depending on who touched the file that day.

David was working as the most expensive secretary in Buffalo, personally involved in every decision because "only I know how to do it right." Rich could see the problems, but couldn't fix them because there were no systematic approaches to fall back on.

The chaos this created was spectacular. One paralegal's "intake" meant three sticky notes and a voicemail. Another had her own system that only she could decipher. And Rich? He was stepping in constantly to "just make sure it was done right." Spoiler: That's not a process. That's chaos with lipstick.

Sound familiar?

The breakthrough came when they finally admitted that yes, they could systematize the routine work. Once they started documenting workflows (how intake should proceed, how medical records were requested, how settlement packets were assembled), the chaos began to calm down.

Results after six months of documented processes: 30 percent faster turnaround times, 15 percent improvement in client satisfaction scores, and they eliminated most of the errors that used to require David's personal firefighting.

The Six to Ten Core Processes That Run Your Firm

David and Rich discovered, and what every firm discovers when it finally gets honest about its operations, that every law firm runs on a handful of core processes. Six to ten, maybe. That's it.

These aren't thousands of detailed steps. They're the major actions that make your business function.

HR Process: How you recruit, hire, onboard, train, and manage people. Right now, you probably do this differently every time. One new hire receives a thorough orientation. The next one gets pointed toward their desk and told to "ask questions if you need help." No wonder you're frustrated with new team members.

Marketing Process: How you generate leads and build your reputation. Some months, you're active on social media. Other months, crickets. Sometimes you follow up with referral sources. Sometimes you forget. No process means no consistency, and the result is no predictable pipeline.

Sales Process: How you convert leads into clients. Do you have a standard initial consultation process? A consistent engagement letter workflow? Please tell me you have a Fee Agreement. A reliable way to collect retainers? Double-please tell me you are using retainers! Or does it depend on who's available that day and how they're feeling?

Operating Processes: How you deliver your legal services. This is where lawyers get most defensive. "Every case is unique!" Sure. But every PI case follows a similar intake, medical records process, demand letter sequence, and settlement procedure. Every estate plan follows a predictable questionnaire, drafting, review, and signing process. Every corporate transaction has standard due diligence steps. You might have a few different operating processes if you have different practice areas or handle substantially different types of cases.

Accounting Process: How you track time, send bills, collect payments, and manage your finances. You'd think this would be standardized by now, but I've seen firms where three different people enter time three different ways, and nobody knows why collections are terrible.

Customer Service Process: How you keep clients informed, handle their calls, and manage their expectations. This one varies wildly in most firms. Some clients get weekly updates. Others hear from you twice in six months and wonder if you're still alive.

Look at that list. Six processes. That's what makes your firm run. Not sixty. Not six hundred. Six to ten major processes that, if you could get them done the right and best way every time, would create consistency and scalability in your firm.

When David and Rich sat down with their leadership team and mapped out what actually happened versus what they thought happened, the gap was alarming. They realized they had to nail down the basics. How does a client get scheduled? Who checks conflicts? Who sets up the file? What happens when medical records come in? Who reviews them? What gets flagged for attorney attention?

These aren't glamorous conversations, but once they're written down, the whole firm exhales. Suddenly, there was a right way. And everybody knew it.

Rich had seen this transformation at a previous firm. "I saw how, if you implement the right processes and procedures, you can effectively manage growth," he explained. "When we found EOS, David and I built the systems around my knowledge base, but in a manner that addressed the shortcomings of other firms."

What "Documenting Your Processes" Really Means

When I say "document your processes," you immediately picture some nightmare scenario: a 700-page standard operating procedures manual that nobody will ever read, nobody will ever follow, and will be outdated before you finish writing it.

That's not what this is. That is a monumental waste of time, money, and effort.

EOS uses a 20/80 approach to documenting processes. You focus on 20 percent of the major steps to get you 80 percent of the way there. Just the major steps. The critical decision points. The things that absolutely have to happen in the right order for the process to work.

Focus on 20 percent of the major steps to get you 80 percent of the way there.

You're not documenting every single mouse click. You're not writing instructions for people who can't think. You're creating a high-level roadmap that shows the right and best way to do something.

Here's what this looked like for David and Rich when they finally documented their personal injury intake and medical records process.

Their Old "System" (existed only in David's head):

- Client calls after an accident

- Someone schedules them somehow

- Consultation happens eventually

- Medical records get requested, maybe

- Documents come in whenever

- Settlement packet gets assembled by whoever has time

- David reviews everything because "only I know how to do it right"

Their New Documented Process (actual major steps):
Medical Records Request Process:

- Receive signed authorization from client within 24 hours of case acceptance (Responsibility: Intake coordinator)

- Send records request to all treating providers within 3 business days (Responsibility: Case manager)

- Follow up if no response within 15 days (Responsibility: Case manager)

- Review records upon receipt for completeness and missing treatment (Responsibility: Paralegal)

- Draft medical summary, flag unusual findings, gaps in treatment, or inconsistencies for attorney review (Responsibility: Paralegal)

- File complete records in case management system with summary note (Responsibility: Paralegal)

Six steps. That's the difference between David personally reviewing every single medical record request (which he was doing before) and his team handling all routine requests independently.

The process wasn't complicated. It answered the most important questions: What happens? In what order? Who's responsible? What does "right" look like?

Notice what's not in there: detailed instructions on how to interpret complex medical findings, nuanced analysis of causation issues, or strategy decisions about which records to emphasize at trial. That's the 20 percent that requires David or Rich's legal expertise. The process documents the 80 percent that needs to happen the same way every time for clients to receive consistent, high-quality service.

Before they documented this process, David and Rich personally reviewed 40-plus medical record requests per week. Every single one. Because they didn't trust that their team would catch problems or know what to flag. After the documented process, the team handled routine requests independently and flagged only the 5–8 per week that genuinely required their expertise.

"The Accountability Chart is the most important thing to get right because it has your biggest day-to-day impact," David told me. "Before, I would say 16 people were coming to my door. Now I'm down to 11, and within the next year and a half, I think I'll be down to four to six."

That's not about avoiding people. That's about building a firm where the systems work so well that people only come to you when something truly requires your expertise.

This is true for every practice area.

Personal Injury Practice (like David and Rich's firm)

- *Routine 80 percent:* Intake process, medical record requests, insurance communication, settlement calculations

- *Expert 20 percent:* Case strategy, complex negotiations, trial preparation, unusual liability issues

Estate Planning Practice

- *Routine 80 percent:* Client questionnaires, document drafting, signing appointments, filing procedures

- *Expert 20 percent:* Complex tax planning, unusual family situations, business succession strategies

Corporate Law Practice
- *Routine 80 percent:* Intake process, standard contract review, filing procedures, client status updates

- *Expert 20 percent:* Complex deal structures, unusual provisions, negotiation strategy, regulatory analysis

Immigration Practice
- *Routine 80 percent:* Form completion, document gathering, filing procedures, status updates

- *Expert 20 percent:* Unusual cases, appeals, complex eligibility analysis, policy interpretation

Family Law Practice
- *Routine 80 percent:* Initial intake and retainer collection, financial disclosure requests, standard parenting plan preparation, court filings, and deadlines

- *Expert 20 percent:* High-conflict custody strategy, complex asset division, negotiation tactics, trial preparation

Once you see this pattern, you can't unsee it. The work you thought was 100 percent unique is, in fact, 80 percent repeatable, with 20 percent that truly requires your expertise.

Followed By All: Where the Real Magic Happens

Here's the thing about documented processes: they're worthless if nobody follows them.

I can't tell you how many firms I've worked with that had process documents. Beautiful binders. Detailed flowcharts. Comprehensive procedures. All gathering dust while everyone continued doing things their own way.

Documentation is only the first tool. The second tool is what EOS calls "Followed By All" (FBA). This is the mechanism that ensures everyone in your organization who touches each process has been properly trained, knows the right way to do things, and is measured and managed to continue to do it the right way every single time.

This is what creates consistency and scalability. Not the documentation. The discipline of faithfully following what you documented.

This is where most law firms fall apart. They're great at documentation. They're terrible at follow-through.

The firms that succeed with processes don't just create them; they also use them. They build them into the fabric of how work gets done. New hires get trained on the processes during onboarding. Team meetings include process reviews. Performance conversations reference whether people are following documented procedures. The processes become part of the firm's operating system, not just documents in a folder somewhere.

Here's the truth: Documented processes sitting in a binder are worthless. Documented processes that everyone has been trained on, understands, and faithfully follows? That's what creates consistency and scalability.

This is what produces the transformation David and Rich experienced. Not the documentation itself, but the discipline of following what they documented. Turnaround times improved. Errors dropped. Client satisfaction increased. But the biggest change? David and Rich weren't answering the same questions over and over anymore.

That's the power of processes that are truly FBA. You move from being the answer to every question to being the exception handler. People follow the process for routine situations. They only come to you when something truly unusual happens.

Rich explained the transformation: "The process that we have in place is game-changing for us. It gives us a leg up on the competition, gives us a leg up on hiring. Every possible aspect of our business is improving because of the systems that we have in place."

The ROI You Can't Ignore

Let's talk about money. I own a fractional CFO company. I love to talk about money because that's what makes this real.

When David and Rich implemented their processes, they tracked the impact. Not because they're nerds (okay, maybe David a little), but because they wanted to know if this was working.

Time savings: David calculated he was spending about 15 hours per week personally reviewing work that could have been handled by his team if they'd had clear processes. That's 60 hours per month. At an effective billing rate of $1,500 per hour (it's actually higher, but let's leave it at that), that's $90,000 in potential productive time he was wasting on internal chaos. Per month. Do the math on that annually and try not to have a small heart attack. David almost did when I showed him similar math one day.

Quality improvement: Before processes, they were catching errors after the fact. Missing deadlines. Forgetting follow-ups. Inconsistent client communication. Each error costs time to fix and erodes client trust. After the processes, their error rate dropped drastically. Not because people got smarter, but because the process caught mistakes before they became problems.

Team confidence: This was the surprising benefit. Once people had clear processes to follow, they stopped being tentative and started being confident. They knew what "right" looked like. They didn't need constant reassurance. Junior team members became productive faster because they had clear guidance and expectations instead of having to figure everything out through trial and error. And remember, Rich and David are growing exponentially every month. They are constantly hiring new people.

Growth capacity: Before processes, David and Rich couldn't grow. They were maxed out. Every new case meant more chaos because there was no system to handle it. After processes, they could take on significantly more cases with the same team size. Because the system could handle it.

Rich told me something that still sticks with me: "We hit our yearly revenue numbers basically halfway through the year. We never would have done that if EOS hadn't been implemented."

But here's the ROI that nobody talks about: firm value. When you go to sell your firm someday (and you will, whether that's in 3 years or 30), documented processes are worth real money. Firms with systematized operations are worth 15–25 percent more than comparable firms where everything lives in the owner's head. Because buyers know they're getting a business, not just buying your personal expertise.

Think about it from a buyer's perspective. Would you rather acquire:

- Firm A: "The owner knows how everything works. You'll need to shadow him for a while to learn the systems."

- Firm B: "Here are our documented processes for everything. The team is trained and follows them consistently. You can review them before the sale."

Which one feels less risky? Which one would you pay more for?

Building a Process-Oriented Culture

Building a culture where everyone cares about processes is the part that takes the longest and matters the most.

Building a culture where everyone cares about processes is the part that takes the longest and matters the most.

Not just mindlessly following processes. Sincerely caring about them. Thinking about them. Improving them.

David and Rich discovered this evolution. First, they had to convince people to follow the processes. That was hard. People resisted. "This feels rigid." "This isn't how I do things." "Can't I just..."

No. Follow the process.

Once people got used to following the processes, something interesting happened. They started suggesting improvements. "Hey, step four in our intake process doesn't make sense. What if we did this instead?" That's when you know it's working, when your team takes ownership of the processes.

Here's how to build this culture.

Start with process ownership: Assign someone to own each core process. Not to micromanage it, but to be responsible for keeping it current, training new people on it, and gathering feedback to improve it. A good idea is to have department heads own specific processes. They became the go-to people for questions and champions of improving processes.

Create feedback loops: Review each process every quarter or two. What's working? What's not? What's changed in the business that requires updating the process? This keeps processes from becoming outdated artifacts.

Celebrate process compliance: When someone follows the process and gets a great result, make noise about it. "Sarah handled the Martinez case perfectly. Followed our process step by step. The client was thrilled. That's what we're aiming for." Positive reinforcement beats criticism every time.

Address resistance directly: Some people will resist. Usually, your highest performers who think rules don't apply to them. Have the conversation. "I know you've been doing this your way for years. And your way works. But we need everyone to do it the same way so we can scale. I need you on board with this."

Connect processes to issues: Remember Chapter 9 and the IDS process? Issues stem from two places: People or Process. When you solve a process issue, turn the solution into a process update. This is how your processes evolve from good to great.

The hardest part about building a process culture in a law firm? Lawyers are trained to think independently. To find unique solutions. To be creative problem solvers. All of that is valuable for the 20 percent of work that requires expertise. But for the 80 percent that's routine? You need consistency, not creativity.

You need consistency, not creativity.

Here's a great way to reframe it: "Processes aren't about limiting your thinking. They're about freeing your thinking. When you don't have to waste mental energy on routine decisions, you have more capacity for the complex work that actually requires your expertise."

Rich put it perfectly when he told me, "We don't have to reinvent the wheel every month like we used to. Almost every month, we would have to sit down and replan how we were going to deal with the growth. Now the systems handle it."

Your Firm Now Has a Scalable Foundation

You now have the processes that make your firm truly scalable. You've documented the core processes that run your business. You've implemented "Followed By All" to ensure consistent execution. You've built a culture where processes are valued and continuously improved.

David and Rich went from chaos to consistency in about six months. Not because they're special, but because they followed the system. They admitted their work wasn't as unique as they thought it was. They documented the 80 percent, trained their team, and held people accountable.

The result? David's bottleneck problem became solvable. Fewer people stand in line to ask him questions. That's not about avoiding people. That's about building a firm that doesn't require constant owner intervention because the systems work.

Rich can now focus on what he loves: taking cases to trial and getting verdicts. "Running the business has definitely taken away my ability to go to court and try cases. EOS will give me the time to do that properly, instead of worrying about cross-examination while simultaneously worrying about who's paying the electric bill and whether or not the copy guy's coming on Tuesday."

Your processes give you freedom. Freedom to focus on complex legal work. Freedom to develop business. Freedom to take a vacation without your phone exploding. Freedom to grow without drowning in chaos.

But having great systems isn't enough. You need the discipline to execute them consistently. Week after week. Quarter after quarter.

Here's what I've seen happen: Firms build great systems and then slowly stop using them. They get lazy about processes. The high standards start to slip, and clients notice. Five-star reviews drop, referrals drop, growth slows down or halts, and eventually, great people leave.

You have vision, the right people, clear data, systematic issue resolution, and documented processes. Now comes the most critical piece: the discipline to execute consistently.

In the next chapter, I'll show you how to create the traction that makes everything else work. Because vision without traction is hallucination, and you didn't come this far to hallucinate.

Chapter Eleven

How to Make EOS Stick in Your Firm

You have all the pieces: vision, people, data, issue resolution, and processes. But here's the brutal reality that separates successful firms from the rest: having the system isn't enough. You need the discipline to execute it consistently.

"Vision Without Traction Is Hallucination"

This saying is something Gino Wickman, the founder of EOS, likes to repeat frequently. And he's right. A beautiful plan that never gets implemented is just a hallucination you wasted time writing on a whiteboard.

This is the trap so many attorneys can't seem to avoid. They love the planning retreats, the grand strategies, the "someday we'll" lists. They leave January off-sites with fancy binders and big intentions. And by February? The binder is on a shelf gathering dust, the team is back to firefighting, and essentially, nothing has changed.

Welcome to the execution gap: the massive gulf between knowing what to do and actually doing it.

Let's use a boat metaphor. Vision plus people plus traction is everyone rowing in sync, working as one body, and getting somewhere instead of just having good intentions. Without traction, you know where you want to go; everyone's rowing in the same direction, but you're still flailing without rhythm.

Traction requires ongoing discipline, not a one-time implementation.

Why is traction the hardest pillar? It requires ongoing discipline, not a one-time implementation. It fights human nature because we default to chaos when pressure increases. It demands accountability because you must measure and confront performance gaps. And it needs leadership commitment because partners and leaders must model the behavior consistently.

Lin McCraw from McCraw Law Group learned this lesson about discipline the hard way. When his lawyers resisted the weekly meeting cadence and didn't follow the process properly, their Rock completion suffered. Lin watched some departments struggle while others thrived. The difference? The departments where leaders didn't think the Level 10 Meetings were important. "The areas where we struggle are those in which people don't think those Level 10s were as important. So maybe they're not following it the way they should."

Lin's response was to stay unwavering about the discipline. As he puts it: "The system works, but only if you work the system." He told his team, "You follow the process, you will get results. But you have to be dogged about following the process. You have to have people at the top who are saying, 'We are going to follow these processes as a firm.'"

And Lin has consistently worked the system. In the five years since he started EOS, his firm has grown from about $2.5 million in revenue to an expected $15 million this year. That kind of growth doesn't happen by accident. It happens through the discipline of traction.

Now here's what EOS teaches about traction: there are two tools that make it work. The first is Rocks. The second is The Meeting Pulse®. Let's start with Rocks.

Rocks: The Discipline of Quarterly Execution

Remember back in Chapter 6 when we talked about the V/TO and one of the Eight Questions was Rocks? Rocks are the three to seven most important things that need to get done this quarter. The question is: how do you continue to execute on them quarter after quarter without losing focus?

That's where traction comes in.

Mike Smith discovered the difference between knowing about Rocks and meticulously completing them. Before EOS, he tried strategic planning. "We would try to do these strategic planning exercises, and we might have a great meeting in January. And then by February, we completely lost sight of whatever it was, whatever we had said were our priorities." Sound familiar?

The problem wasn't that Mike didn't know what to do. He'd read the books, been through the coaching programs. "The concepts of strategic planning and Rocks and having priorities that you would set at the forefront of everything, those were not new concepts to me."

But knowledge without execution is just expensive entertainment.

What changed for Mike? The weekly accountability. "We're looking at those priorities every week. And that alone just... just the discipline with your leadership team around looking at these priorities and making sure that they stay the priority."

Mike's first completed Rock? Signing 90 clients in a quarter. "We signed up over 30 clients each month. That was huge from a revenue perspective. And it represented a new threshold. So that felt great."

That win built confidence. Then came another completed Rock. And another. Before long, Mike's team stopped doubting whether Rocks would get done. They expected completion because they'd built the discipline to make it happen.

The 90-Day World isn't about what you write down in your quarterly planning session. It's about what you systematically execute on through weekly discipline. Every week, you check your Rocks. Are they on track? Off track? What issues are blocking completion? What needs to happen this week to move them forward?

That's the pulse that creates traction. Not the planning. The execution.

And here's the kicker about the power of this pulse: Remember Lin, who built that family-owned law firm so quickly? After his initial turnover when he implemented EOS, Lin's firm has maintained very low employee turnover despite massive growth. The system became bigger than any individual person. New leaders got plugged into the 90-Day World immediately. They learned the language, understood the expectations, and started executing from day one. The Rocks give them clear priorities. The quarterly pulse gives them structure. The accountability gives them confidence.

That's the power of execution discipline.

The Meeting Pulse®: Your Execution Engine

Now let's talk about the second tool that makes traction work: The Meeting Pulse.

Most law firms think meetings are about sharing information. Wrong. Meetings are about creating momentum.

Meetings are about creating momentum.

The Meeting Pulse isn't just a calendar of recurring appointments. It's your execution rhythm. Consistency creates momentum. Regular rhythm builds execution habits. Weekly check-ins prevent drift. And frequent touch points keep everyone rowing in the same direction.

The Meeting Pulse has layers.

Annual Planning: This is your visioning session where you clarify or refine your 10-Year Target, 3-Year Picture, and 1-Year Plan. You review Core Values, identify major initiatives, and align on the big picture for the coming year.

Quarterly Sessions: The 90-Day World® :Every quarter, you assess the previous quarter's performance, solve the big issues that emerged, and set new 90-day priorities (Rocks) for each person. This is where you adjust course and maintain momentum. You celebrate what got done. You analyze what didn't. You recalibrate your priorities based on reality.

Weekly Level 10 Meetings: This is the heartbeat of EOS execution. Ninety minutes, same agenda every week. These prevent problems from becoming crises and remove roadblocks to keep up the momentum.

Daily Huddles: These are not part of EOS, but are 10-minute team check-ins for immediate coordination and quick issue flagging. Some firms do these, others find weekly Level 10 Meetings sufficient.

The magic isn't in the individual meetings. It's in the pulse. Week after week, quarter after quarter, your team builds muscle memory for execution. They stop waiting for you to tell them what to do and start owning their results.

Mike Griffin and Chuck Welsh from Griffin Welsh, P.A., run two separate companies. When they learned they needed weekly Level 10 Meetings for each company, Chuck's immediate reaction was resistance. Three hours of meetings per week? Chuck gets up at 5:30, works out, gets to the office, and doesn't leave until 6:30 or 7:00. "Really, you're going to tell me, as busy as I am, that I'm going to spend 90 full minutes on each company?"

Time is money for lawyers who bill by the hour. The idea of dedicating six hours per week to meetings felt like it would kill productivity.

But they committed to the discipline anyway.

The first quarter felt forced. The meetings happened, but Chuck and Mike weren't convinced this was worth the time investment. By the second quarter, something shifted. The weekly pulse started revealing patterns. Issues that used to bounce around for weeks got resolved in 90 minutes. Problems got caught before they became crises. The team stopped coming to Chuck and Mike for every decision because they had clarity on priorities and ownership.

"Getting through the first quarter and then starting to think about what was going to be our presentation to the firm about where we were and getting the discipline ourselves of doing these meetings," Chuck said. "It was probably midway through the second quarter where I would have said this is actually working and I'm starting to believe that this is a good process."

The weekly meetings that seemed like a time drain? Now they create time. "Time is money," Chuck acknowledged. "But if they're creating more billable work for people and we're figuring out how to be more efficient, it's worth it."

That's the power of The Meeting Pulse. The rhythm doesn't consume time. It creates it. By solving problems systematically every week, you eliminate the hours spent firefighting. By maintaining clear priorities, you stop wasting time on things that don't matter. By holding people accountable weekly, you prevent the drift that kills momentum.

The Meeting Pulse isn't about having more meetings. It's about having the right meetings, with the right structure and at the right frequency, to create predictable execution.

The Level 10 Meeting: Where Everything Happens

Let me walk you through what makes a Level 10 Meeting different from every other waste-of-time meeting you've ever attended.

First, same day, same time, same agenda every single week. Non-negotiable. This isn't a meeting you move when something "more important" comes up. This IS the most important thing. Because this is where you ensure everything else actually gets done.

Second, they start on time and end on time. They last 90 minutes. Not two hours. Not "until we're done." Exactly 90 minutes. Chuck's firm found that some weeks they don't need the full time. "Some weeks you come in, and we don't have 15 issues, which is okay. So let's get through what we have. Let's end the meeting early, and let's move on." That's fine. The discipline is showing up every week.

Third, the agenda[1] is standardized and time-boxed. See the diagram on page 138.

It is broken into a few sections. The Segue gets everybody focused, then the next few parts are all about reporting. Is everything on track with your Scorecard numbers, your Rocks, are there any Headlines somebody needs to announce, and then did the To Dos get to done? None of this requires discussion. It's why these sections are only allotted 5 minutes each.

Mike Griffin's COO, Chantel, learned to run their Level 10 Meetings and became excellent at keeping them on track. "She's very good at bringing us back to focus and not allowing us to pontificate and, you know, not allowing us to go here, there, and everywhere because that was how the L10^{TM} would work out before. We would just talk and talk and talk, and we weren't doing a true IDS process."

The IDS methodology comes from Chapter 9. You **Identify** the real root cause by digging beyond the symptom. You **Discuss** it briefly with nobody repeating themselves. Then you **Solve** it permanently. Solve generally means somebody commits to doing something by a certain date. This usually looks like a To Do. Chuck nailed why this works: "By being disciplined enough every week to put something on there that's an issue, that then creates to-dos that get things done. We didn't have that kind of discipline before."

The vast majority of the meeting (60 minutes of a 90-minute meeting) is spent solving problems, not discussing them or complaining about them, or analyzing them to death. You're using the IDS methodology from Chapter 9 to solve issues at the root.

Here's where technology becomes your accountability partner. When you're running L10s on software like **Strety**, the agenda isn't just a sug-

---

1. To learn more about the L10 Agenda and how to run the meeting, go to www.EOSWorldw ide.com/Level-10

gestion; it's built into the platform with timers that keep each section on track. This matters more than you might think, especially as you push L10s deeper into the firm. Your leadership team might have the discipline to stay on agenda. But what about department meetings? What about the team three levels down that's never run a structured meeting in their lives?

Without structure, those meetings drift. People skip sections. The IDS portion shrinks to 15 minutes because someone spent 40 minutes on the Segue talking about their kid's soccer tournament. And here's the hard truth: Sloppy L10s give you lazy accountability, which gives you lousy results. The whole point of pushing EOS through the firm is to get everyone rowing in the same direction, but that only works if everyone is running the system the way it was designed.

Strety keeps people honest. The timer creates gentle pressure to move through each section. The standardized agenda means a department head can't decide to "customize" the meeting into something unrecognizable. And because everything, Issues, to-dos, Rocks, The Accountability Chart, and VTO, lives in one connected system, there's visibility. Leadership can see whether meetings are happening, whether issues are getting solved, and whether the discipline is holding. It's not micromanagement. It's making sure your investment in EOS pays off at every level.

Level 10 Meetings create the weekly pulse that keeps everyone aligned. But weekly meetings are only half the accountability equation. You also need a culture where accountability feels like support, not punishment. Where people want to perform well rather than just avoid getting in trouble.

> **Level 10 meetings create the weekly rhythm that keep everyone aligned.**

Creating a Culture of Accountability

Most law firms think accountability means catching people doing things wrong and calling them out. They think it's about consequences and discipline, and performance improvement plans.

That's not accountability. That's fear-based management. And it doesn't work.

Real accountability means people taking personal ownership of results, not just activity. It means transparent performance where everyone knows how they and others are doing. It means mutual support where team members help each other succeed. And it means honest conversations that address performance gaps directly but kindly.

The problem? Law firms face unique accountability challenges that make this harder than it sounds.

- **Partnership dynamics** create peer-to-peer accountability instead of traditional hierarchy. You can't just fire a partner who's not performing.

- **Billable-hour focus** trains everyone to think about time spent instead of results achieved.

- **Individual-contributor mindset** means lawyers are trained to work independently, not collaboratively.

- And **ego management** is a constant issue because high-achieving professionals resist being managed.

So how do you build accountability systems that actually work?

Clear expectations. Everyone knows what success looks like. Not vague goals like "be a team player" or "improve client service." Implement specific, measurable expectations tied to Core Values, Rocks, and Measurables.

Regular check-ins. Not annual performance reviews. Consistent rhythm of performance conversations. Weekly in Level 10 Meetings for tactical updates. Quarterly for deeper development discussions.

Data-driven discussions. Numbers remove emotion from accountability. "Your client satisfaction score dropped from 9.2 to 8.4 this quarter" is a fact, not an attack. It opens a conversation about what changed and how to fix it.

Consequences and rewards. Both positive and negative outcomes for performance. But here's the critical part: the focus must be on making accountability positive, not punitive.

Development focus. Help people improve, don't just criticize. When someone's struggling, the question isn't "Why are you failing?" It's "What support do you need to succeed?"

Recognition and celebration. Acknowledge good performance publicly. Lawyers are terrible at this. We notice problems immediately and rarely celebrate wins. Flip that ratio.

Resource provision. Give people the tools and support they need to succeed. Don't hold someone accountable for results if you haven't given them what they need to achieve those results.

Growth opportunities. Connect performance to career advancement. Show people how meeting expectations leads to bigger opportunities. Make accountability feel like a path forward, not a trap.

That's the foundation. Now let me show you how to put these principles into practice with each person on your team.

The Quarterly Conversation: Accountability in Action

To maintain accountability, you need to have a way to meet with your direct reports and make sure expectations are clear, both yours and theirs. EOS has a Tool for this called Quarterly Conversations[2]. The Quarterly Conversation is just as it sounds, a simple conversation between you and your direct reports. This replaces complicated performance reviews that go in an employee's file with an open and honest conversation. What's working, what's not working, can the not-working items be fixed, and what is each of you going to do to improve the relationship? It is a two-way conversation with input and suggestions from both sides.

Done well, Quarterly Conversations reduce turnover, build trust, and catch problems early. The 90-day rhythm means course correction happens fast. And the mutual accountability shows your team that everyone, including you, has room to improve.

This is accountability as support, not punishment. This is how you build a culture where people feel valued and heard, not just managed and evaluated.

Integrating All EOS Tools for Maximum Impact

The beautiful thing about EOS is that each component is powerful on its own. But when they all work together? That's when the real transformation happens.

Mike Smith's estate planning firm demonstrates this integration perfectly. Revenue grew from $1.2 million to a projected $5 million in less

---

2. To learn more about Quarterly Conversations, go to www.EOSWorldwide.com/Quarterly
-Conversations

than two years. His entire original leadership team turned over, yet the firm kept executing. He launched a registered investment advisory firm, is starting a coaching program for estate planning attorneys, and took an equity stake in an AI company. And here's the kicker: "I've been doing this for over 30 years, and my level of excitement about my firm has never been higher."

That kind of transformation doesn't come from implementing one tool. It comes from the integration of all Six Key Components working together like a Swiss watch.

Vision drives everything. On Mike's V/TO, his 10-Year Target gave him direction: "Build a strong, enduring firm where leadership and opportunity expand beyond the founders." Every other tool serves that vision. His quarterly Rocks move him toward it. His people decisions support it. His processes enable it.

People execute the vision. Mike had to make tough calls. He even had to have a tough conversation with his partner. Twice. Once to step down from the leadership team, and then another time when it was time to stop practicing law. But at the same time, his new hiring process was bringing in great team members to the firm's staff and keeping it growing.

Data shows progress. Mike tracks client satisfaction through a disguised survey system built into every client interaction. He monitors cash flow weekly using forecasting tools. "That has given me some peace because we didn't have a good way to track that before." The Scorecard numbers tell him proactively when there's a problem instead of waiting for clients to complain.

Issues remove obstacles. Mike's team solves problems systematically in their weekly Level 10 Meetings. No more "barely contained chaos" where everything depends on him. "I look at things now as a business problem, and we need to address the issue and figure out how to solve it. Whereas in the past, I kind of looked at our practice as limiting from a growth and financial standpoint."

Processes create consistency. Before EOS, Mike had "a bunch of mini-mes" doing task delegation. Now his team takes ownership of projects. The processes ensure quality without Mike personally touching everything.

Traction maintains discipline. Weekly accountability around Rocks. Quarterly planning sessions. A Meeting Pulse that never stops. "If we didn't have the weekly meeting cadence and the quarterly planning meetings and the accountability through the Scorecard, we'd be right back where we were. I would be at the center of everything."

Watch how these components integrate in Mike's typical quarter:

Annual planning sets the vision and financial goals. Mike knows where he's going: build a sellable firm that doesn't depend on him.

Quarterly Rocks break that vision into 90-day priorities. Sign 90 new clients. Launch the RIA. Build the coaching program. Specific, measurable, achievable this quarter.

Weekly meetings keep everything on track. Review the Scorecard. Check Rock progress. IDS the issues that come up. Assign to-dos. Rate the meeting. Next week, do it again.

Daily execution happens through documented processes. The team knows what to do. They don't need Mike for routine decisions. They only escalate true exceptions.

Continuous improvement happens naturally. Issues surface in meetings. Data reveals problems early. Processes get refined. The system gets better every quarter.

The compound effect is simple but profound: Each tool makes the others work better. Vision guides Rocks. Rocks get tracked in meetings. Meetings drive accountability. Accountability feeds into people decisions and process improvements. Issues get solved instead of recycled. Data ties it all together.

> **Each tool makes the others work better.**

Mike saw this when he made his first tough people decision about asking his partner to step off the leadership team. "The process of EOS, the process of those L10 Meetings, everything we'd done in our focus day; that gave us the confidence to know it was the right thing to do." The system supported the hard choice.

Individual tools are helpful. Vision without traction is hallucination. People without processes can't scale. Data without action is just noise. But the integrated system? Transformative.

Mike put it perfectly: "If people aren't aligned with the values of the firm, they're not invested. And if we didn't have EOS anymore, I think it would be nearly impossible to manage what we've grown. It's just too big now for me to keep track of it all."

That's the whole point. The system becomes bigger than any individual, including the owner. Sustained discipline creates momentum. Consistency builds on itself. And over time, the team becomes self-managing and accountable.

Mike's transformation yielded dramatic results in less than a year. And here's what he discovered: it's not magic. It's discipline. It's showing up every week. It's following the process even when it feels awkward. It's trusting the system.

And when you do? "The sky's the limit in terms of how much we can grow."

LEVEL 10 MEETING®

Day: _________________________________   Time: _________________________________

AGENDA

Segue	5	Minutes
Scorecard	5	Minutes
Rock Review	5	Minutes
Customer/Employ	5	Minutes
To-Do List	5	Minutes
IDS®	60	Minutes
Conclude	5	Minutes

Conclude
    Recap To-Do List
    Cascading Messages
    Rating (1-10)

Part 3: Sustaining Success

Chapter Twelve

But What If It Won't Work for Me?

You now understand the complete Entrepreneurial Operating System and how to execute it with discipline. You've seen how Rocks create 90-day focus. You know why The Meeting Pulse matters. You understand that vision without traction is hallucination.

But I can already hear what you're thinking: "This sounds great, Brooke, but my firm is different. My practice area is unique. My situation is special. This probably won't work for me."

I've heard every version of this objection. "We're too small." "We're too big." "Law is different from other businesses." "Our clients won't tolerate systems." "Lawyers are too independent." "We've tried this stuff before and it didn't work."

And here's the truth: Every single lawyer I've worked with had these exact same doubts. These concerns are normal, valid, and completely understandable.

They're also completely wrong.

Not because your situation isn't unique (it is). Not because implementing EOS is easy (it's not). But because the fundamental principles of running a business systematically apply regardless of your size, your practice area, or your history.

Let me prove it by going back to two of the most skeptical attorneys I've ever met.

The Ultimate Skeptics

Remember Mike Griffin and Chuck Welsh from Chapter 9, the partners running ACCEL Law Group in West Hartford who were stuck in perpetual firefighting mode? Mike was buried under that deli-counter line of staff outside his door, while Chuck was frustrated by the same five or six chronic problems cropping up every single month.

Here's what I didn't tell you before: When they first heard about EOS, they were the definition of skeptical.

Chuck's immediate reaction? "Do I want to spend time learning to do something else? I've got 14 hours a day of stuff I can do." Even hearing it called the Entrepreneurial Operating System made him skeptical. "What is that? What does that mean?"

Mike was slightly more open but still doubted they had the bandwidth. "The bigger concern was we're too busy to spend time working on the business. We're busy. We have clients. We're succeeding. We're making money."

Their first attempt at EOS came through a consulting group that promoted a "modified" version. Not Certified EOS Implementers. Just consultants with good intentions who combined some great tools from the book with other things they had learned over the years. Mike and Chuck spent two years in that half-committed state, and it didn't work. Chuck lost interest. "I was more of the viewpoint, I don't know that this is going to work." The process felt unprepared, the meetings felt forced, and worst of all, they'd tried to include everyone in the firm from day one. Eight people sitting in a room, half of them thinking, "I could be billing time right now."

They were about to walk away from the whole thing.

Then they were approached by a Certified EOS Implementer®. After hearing his pitch, they said, "Let's actually start with the beginning of the book. Let's understand what these phases are and what they mean." This time, they committed to doing it right. Full implementation. Proper process. Real discipline.

Chuck's skepticism didn't disappear overnight. Remember from Chapter 11 when they learned they'd need weekly Level 10 Meetings for both companies? That guy who gets up at 5:30 a.m., works out, gets to the office, and doesn't leave until 6:30 or 7:00? Three hours of meetings per week felt like productivity suicide.

When they actually committed to the system, the first quarter felt forced. By the second quarter, something shifted. Midway through that quarter, Chuck had his breakthrough moment. "This is actually working. I'm starting to believe that this is a good process."

The issues that used to take weeks to resolve? Getting solved in weekly meetings. The deli-counter line outside Mike's door? Gone. The chronic problems that had been plaguing them for years? Systematically eliminated through the IDS process.

Chuck, the skeptic who almost walked away entirely, now tells other doubting attorneys: "We thought we had some things figured out, but we didn't have the processes and structure we needed. If you're thinking what I thought, that this is just corporate nonsense or a time suck, you need to try it. Because the alternative is living with the same problems forever."

Belief 1: "My cases are too unique to systematize."

Chuck and Mike specialized in insurance M&A and regulatory work. Complex deals. Unique situations. Every transaction is different. Chuck would pick his favorite attorney next door to handle whatever work came in. No system, just gut feel and relationships. This felt personal, flexible, and sophisticated.

It was also chaos.

"We had to think harder about work allocation and whether or not Mike and I are letting it go, or if it's getting stuck, and we are the blockers," Chuck explained. The "flexibility" was, in fact, creating bottlenecks. Work piled up because only certain people could handle certain things, and Chuck and Mike couldn't keep track of who had capacity.

Then they implemented a triage process that Yulia, one of their senior associates (now counsel), developed for the regulatory group. The moment a regulatory assignment comes in, it goes to a separate triage email. Chuck specifies how much time it should take, who gets billed, and when it's needed. Yulia knows who has the capacity because the three practice group leaders meet regularly to allocate work strategically.

"That's all the stuff I don't think we would have done without bringing more discipline to it through EOS," Chuck admitted. They've now rolled out the same triage process to the corporate and contracts group.

They were shocked that the systematic approach didn't make the work less personal or sophisticated. It made it better. Associates got work that matched their skill level and capacity. Clients got faster turnarounds. Chuck and Mike stopped being bottlenecks. And the 80 percent of work that followed predictable patterns? It got handled efficiently, freeing everyone to focus on the truly complex 20 percent.

Even engagement letters got systematized. Before EOS, Chuck did his own version, Mike did his, and their partner Dan did his. They'd hired a Six Sigma guy to create processes, but nothing ever got implemented. Now? Chuck shoots an email to the paralegal. Five minutes later, he's got an engagement letter ready to send out. Same form as Dan's using. Same form Mike's using. Consistent quality, no reinventing the wheel.

They even systematized conflict checks, which had been entirely in Chuck and Mike's heads. "We have a conflict with this company? No, I don't think we have a conflict. We're good." Not exactly a reliable system for an insurance practice where conflicts matter enormously.

The work is still sophisticated. The deals are still complex. But the 80 percent that can be systematized? Now it runs without Chuck and Mike's constant attention.

Belief 2: "We don't have time for meetings and processes."

Remember from Chapter 11 when Chuck resisted the idea of weekly Level 10 Meetings because of his already long days? That resistance came from somewhere deeper than just schedule pressure.

The assumption was that systems and meetings would consume time rather than create it. Every hour spent in a meeting or documenting a process felt like an hour stolen from billable work or client service. The opposite turned out to be true.

Things that had been sitting on sticky notes on Chuck's desk for months? Suddenly getting resolved. "Issues might have been on a sticky that I got on my desk here that's been just sitting there. I got to do something about that. Now they're getting solved."

The weekly accountability became its own motivator. Nobody wants to show up to a meeting and have Chuck ask, "You didn't do the three things you said you were going to do by this week?" That gentle peer pressure (or as Chuck called it, "kind of close to accountability") proved more effective than any personal to-do list.

The time investment paid compound returns. Problems that used to bounce around for weeks got solved in 90-Minute Meetings. Issues that would have required multiple email threads and sidebar conversations got addressed systematically. Projects that never quite happened because everyone was too busy? They got assigned, tracked, and completed.

"Process has been the biggest change," Chuck concluded. "Getting process, thereby helping me get stuff off my plate, and a process to get important decisions out there, getting people weighing in and then getting past it, resolving it, whatever it might be."

The meetings that felt like a time sink became the best investment in time creation they'd ever made. The processes that seemed like busywork became the foundation for successfully getting things done.

Belief 3: "If I want it done right, I have to do it myself."

I know I keep bringing up Mike's deli-counter problem in Chapter 9. But what drove it wasn't micromanagement for its own sake. He genuinely believed that his involvement ensured quality. He'd built this firm from nothing. He knew every client, understood every deal, and had his finger on every pulse.

"I was clearly a bottleneck because I wanted to be involved and have my hand in everything," Mike admitted. "I wanted to have final decision-making because that's the way we had grown the firm successfully."

This creates a painful paradox. You hire people to help you scale, but then you become the constraint on their effectiveness. Mike saw it clearly: "I was frustrated that people were waiting on me. I'm trying to hold people accountable, and I'm having a hard time holding myself accountable because I'm so busy. It's okay for me to miss a deadline, but I don't want my team to miss deadlines."

The breakthrough came when EOS forced them to define what "done right" actually meant through clear processes and expectations. "If I give you something to do and there's no process, and I don't clearly set the expectation of what I'm hoping you're going to produce, how do you know what you're doing?" Mike realized.

The triage process became the perfect example. Instead of Chuck picking whoever was next door to handle work (his "favorite attorney"), assignments now go through a systematic process. Yulia knows who has the capacity. Work gets distributed based on skill level and availability, not proximity or relationship.

Their weekly data-tracking changed delegation, too. Before EOS, they'd look at billable hours at the end of the month and wonder why someone's billable hours were low. Now they track weekly numbers and can adjust work allocation in real time. "Identifying that was a really critical component; we want to know every week how much revenue is coming in, how much we bill, how each person bills individually," Chuck explained.

Quality didn't drop when Mike stopped being the final decision-maker for everything. It improved because decisions happened faster, work didn't pile up in Mike's queue, and the team had clear standards to work toward. The deli counter is about to close permanently.

Belief 4: "This will make us too corporate and bureaucratic."

Chuck came from LeBoeuf Lamb, a major international law firm in New York. Mike spent years at Edwards & Angell. They'd both lived the big-firm experience with all its meetings, procedures, politics, and red tape. They'd left precisely to escape that bureaucracy and build something nimble and entrepreneurial.

So when EOS came with its formal processes, structured meetings, and documented procedures, Chuck's initial reaction was visceral resistance. "I also didn't like the concept of Rocks, just the whole way it was presented. To me, it was just... I felt like I was in kindergarten. Okay, we're going to get our Rocks now."

The terminology felt cutesy. The structure felt corporate. The whole thing seemed designed for massive organizations, not a specialized insurance law practice trying to stay lean and responsive.

"You know, it's an interesting question because I don't know that you'd ever get an 800-lawyer or 1,200-lawyer firm trying to take this on," Chuck reflected later. "It's not appropriate for them. They're not entrepreneurial."

The irony? EOS made their firm more entrepreneurial, not less.

Before EOS, they operated what Chuck called "a bunch of silos." Each partner did their own thing. Each practice area had its own approach. No shared language, no unified systems, no coordinated strategy. It felt entrepreneurial, but in reality, it was fragmentation dressed up as flexibility.

After EOS, they finally had what Chuck called "operating more as a team." The core values they developed through EOS weren't corporate speak. They were specific, meaningful principles that the team sincerely uses. In their weekly meetings, team members now point out examples of colleagues demonstrating those values. "That means to me it's clicking. People are actually looking for those examples."

The processes didn't create bureaucracy. They created speed. That engagement letter that used to have three partners, each doing a different version? Now it takes five minutes, and it's consistent. The conflict check that used to be whatever Chuck and Mike remembered? Now it's systematic and reliable.

The processes didn't create bureaucracy. They created speed.

"The discipline here is just to get them all out of your head and onto the list," Chuck explained about their Issues List. They're not creating endless meetings to discuss trivial matters. They're capturing everything once and dealing with it systematically.

The structure didn't make them corporate. It made them better.

The Complete Transformation

By the third quarter of implementation, Mike could finally see the compound effect. "I can break it into three quarters," he explained. "At the end of the first quarter, we were kind of exhausted and on very uneasy ground. Like, what did we just do? I just shone the bright light on a lot of our problems and challenges, and this doesn't feel great."

The second quarter brought some stability, but it still felt shaky. "I got to about the middle of May, and all hell's breaking loose. And I called our implementer, and I said, 'Mike Z, what's going on?' And he said, 'This is kind of to be expected. At the end of each quarter, you're going to start to see the stress fractures, but it gets better quarter over quarter.'"

The third quarter was when everything clicked. "This quarter, it's gone much better as we get better at the L10 process. And now I feel like I'm seeing more instances of small evidence of traction. I think this has been the most productive quarter we've ever had. Maybe not on a straight revenue basis, but in terms of forward motion and being more stable."

Chuck shared a message to firms muddling along without systems: "It will be liberating because it'll help you focus on things that you weren't aware you weren't doing well and problems that you may have had."

What would they tell their pre-EOS selves? Simple. Stop waiting. The problems don't fix themselves, and the chaos only gets worse as you grow. "We thought we had some things figured out, but we didn't have the processes and structure we needed."

Mike and Chuck's story proves that even the strongest skeptics can shift their beliefs when the evidence becomes undeniable. They tested their doubts against reality, and the results spoke for themselves.

But here's where the conversation usually shifts. You've seen the evidence. You believe EOS can work. The internal objections have been addressed. Now the practical voice kicks in.

"Sure, this works in theory. But we don't have the time. We don't have the money. Our regulatory environment is too complex. We're too small. The risk is too high."

These external constraints feel more real than internal doubts because they are measurable, visible, and immediate. Unlike beliefs that live in your head, constraints live in your calendar, your bank account, and your state bar requirements. They're not imaginary. They're Tuesday at 3 p.m. when you have no time and a line of people waiting for answers.

The firms that focus on working systematically within their constraints find ways to transform them.

Yes, the constraints are real, but they're not permanent. The firms that focus on working systematically within their constraints find ways to transform them.

The firms that focus on working systematically within their constraints find ways to transform them.

Firms that focus primarily on the constraints themselves tend to get stuck.

In the next chapter, let's tackle those practical concerns head-on and show you how firms are making EOS work not despite their limitations, but because of them.

Chapter Thirteen

Time, Money, and Real Life

"Okay, Brooke. I believe the system works. But my situation is different."

Here come the logistics.

- The calendar that's already maxed out.

- The budget that's already stretched.

- The regulatory environment that adds a complexity you can't simply systematize away.

- The office space that's bursting at the seams.

- The hiring market that makes finding good people nearly impossible.

These aren't beliefs you can talk yourself out of. These are Thursday morning realities staring you in the face.

The constraints are real. I'm not going to tell you they're not. But they're not permanent. There's a massive difference between firms that work systematically within their constraints and firms that let constraints become their identity.

The Constraint Trap

David Wolff wasn't being irrational. He was being practical.

Before EOS, David and his partners, Rich Hall and Joe Nicastro, were managing real limitations at their personal injury practice in Buffalo, rapid growth they weren't prepared for, and office space so cramped that people were working two or three to an office. Rich had given up his office entirely and was working out of whatever conference room was available. Despite all these people crammed together, they were still short-staffed. Hiring in Buffalo isn't easy.

"My excuse for lack of implementation was always a lack of resources," David told me. "We've never had this kind of money before. Is this going to continue? Do we really need somebody to run a marketing department?"

Sound familiar? You see an opportunity, and your first instinct is to evaluate it through your current limitations. You're thinking about time, money, people, and regulations. Being careful with resources that feel scarce.

The challenge is when constraint evaluation becomes the only evaluation. When every opportunity gets filtered through "but we can't becau se..." rather than "how might we...". The opportunity passes, the problem persists, and you prove your constraints were permanent.

Meanwhile, other firms with nearly identical constraints are growing systematically. Not because they have fewer limitations but because they're approaching those limitations differently.

The challenge is when constraint evaluation becomes the only evaluation.

The biggest constraint was time. "I'm not going to be able to do this forever," David realized.

Instead, they chose investment thinking.

"Before I was trying to fix things that happened yesterday," David explained. "Now my decisions are about fixing things six months from now."

The Five Constraint-to-Investment Shifts

Systematic Thinking Framework

Constraint Thinking	Investment Thinking	Result
"We don't have time."	"Systems create time."	Time multiplication
"Too complex/regulated."	"Systems reduce risk."	Compliance confidence
"We're too small."	"Systems scale with us."	Growth foundation
"We can't change our current situation."	"Work within the system"	Resource maximization
"Too risky to change."	"Riskier to stay chaotic."	Strategic advantage

Constraint 1: "We don't have time." → "We don't have time NOT to invest in systems."

David's time scarcity wasn't a perception problem. It was math. Before EOS, he was personally involved in every decision because "only I know how to do it right." The firm had 32 people, and 16 of them regularly came to his door for guidance. Add cramped office space with Rich working out of conference rooms, and you have a recipe for constant interruption.

"I'm not going to be able to keep up this pace forever," David realized.

When you're already working at capacity, where do you find time to implement systems? The idea of adding meetings, planning sessions, and process documentation to an impossible schedule feels overwhelming.

David discovered: systematic thinking creates time rather than consuming it. But it's an investment that pays off over weeks and months, not immediately. Within 90 days of implementing Accountability Charts and clear processes, David went from 16 people coming to his door to 11.

The math is simple. Each person who came to David's door represented 15–20 minutes of interruption and context-switching time. Sixteen interruptions per day meant roughly five hours of reactive problem-solving. By systematically defining roles and creating clear processes, David reclaimed those five hours for strategic work.

David once confided to me that he used to go to bed every night feeling responsible for Laura, his head of Intake. But not any longer. That shift didn't happen by accident. It happened because they invested time in building systems that enabled Laura to own her role fully.

Chuck Welsh from Chapter 12 experienced the same transformation. Remember his resistance to three hours of meetings per week, even though he already worked 14-hour days and questioned if it was worth learning something new?

But systematic issue resolution through Level 10 Meetings created time. Problems that used to bounce around for weeks got solved in 90-minute sessions. The time investment versus time return proved decisive. David spent approximately 40 hours over three months documenting processes and implementing accountability structures. In return, he gained back 20-plus hours per week of strategic time. That's a 1,300 percent return on time investment within the first quarter.

Constraint 2: "Our regulatory environment is too complex." → "Systems reduce compliance risk."

Personal injury practice operates under intense regulatory scrutiny. Client funds must be managed precisely. Case deadlines are court-imposed and non-negotiable. Documentation requirements are extensive. Marketing regulations are strict and constantly evolving.

David and Rich understood this complexity intimately. Rich had been in the legal world "since I was in seventh grade" and had seen firms crumble under regulatory pressure. The natural instinct was to treat regulation as a constraint, something that made systematic approaches risky or impossible.

But they discovered that systematic approaches essentially simplified compliance management. Instead of relying on individual knowledge and memory, the firm created documented processes for trust account management, deadline tracking, client communication, and case documentation.

"I saw how, if you implement the right processes and procedures, you can effectively manage growth," Rich explained. The key insight: systems don't create regulatory risk. They reduce it.

Before EOS, compliance depended on individual vigilance. David might remember that a particular deadline was approaching, or a staff member might catch a discrepancy in a trust account. After EOS, compliance became systematic. Deadlines got tracked automatically. Trust account procedures became standardized and auditable. Client communication followed documented protocols.

Mike Griffin and Chuck Welsh experienced similar levels of compliance confidence in their heavily regulated environment. Their firm operates in both traditional law practice and compliance consulting. As Mike explained in Chapter 12, "We didn't have clear processes, and we didn't have clear expectations. If I give you something to do and there's no process, and I don't clearly set the expectation of what I'm hoping you're going to produce, how do you know what you're doing?"

Systematic approaches created what I call "compliance confidence." The security that comes from knowing your processes consistently meet regulatory requirements, not just when someone remembers to check.

When David's firm implemented systematic deadline tracking, they moved from hoping someone caught important dates to knowing the system would flag them automatically. When they documented trust account procedures, they moved from depending on individual expertise to having auditable processes that any trained team member could follow correctly.

The regulatory environment didn't change. Their systematic approach to managing that environment changed everything.

Constraint 3: "We're too small/specialized." → "Systematic thinking scales with any size."

David and Rich's firm proves that systematic thinking isn't about size. It's about mindset. When they started the EOS implementation, they had fewer than 10 people crammed into inadequate office space. Personal injury practice in Buffalo isn't exactly Fortune 500 territory. Hiring was difficult because the talent pool was limited.

"We would always just be thinking small picture, plug the hole, and thinking that our talent would be able to solve the big picture's problems," David admitted. This is classic small-firm thinking: *We're too small for real systems, we'll just solve problems as they come up, our personal relationships can substitute for formal processes.*

But David learned that systematic thinking is what enables small firms to compete with larger ones. "The Accountability Chart is the most important thing to get right because it has your biggest day-to-day impact." Even with limited people in cramped quarters, clear role definition eliminated confusion and duplication.

Systematic thinking gave them frameworks that scaled with their growth. Instead of reinventing responses to every situation, they had processes that adapted to each situation. When the caseload increased, the intake system absorbed the volume. When they needed to hire, The Accountability Chart showed exactly where new people fit.

Chuck Welsh and Mike Griffin's experience reinforces this. ACCELLaw Group runs both a law practice and a compliance consulting business. Two different service lines that require different expertise. "We're not operating a bunch of silos anymore. We're operating more as a team," Chuck explained. Systematic thinking coordinated complexity rather than adding to it.

Small firms can implement systematic changes faster than large ones.

Mike's perspective captures the shift perfectly. Before EOS: "I've said for decades that law and selling time is a terrible business." After EOS, he owns a business with solvable problems.

The size constraint is frankly an advantage in disguise. Small firms can implement systematic changes faster than large ones. They have fewer people to coordinate, less bureaucracy to navigate, and more flexibility to adapt processes quickly.

Constraint 4: "We can't change our current situation." → "Strategic investment changes everything."

This might be the most insidious constraint because it feels so permanent. David's office space was genuinely cramped. Rich really was working out of conference rooms. Hiring in Buffalo genuinely was difficult. These weren't excuses. They were facts.

The breakthrough came when David and Rich shifted from "We can't change this" to "We can work systematically within this." EOS didn't require them to solve all their space problems before starting. It didn't demand they suddenly find unlimited budget or perfect candidates in a limited talent pool. It required them to work more systematically with what they had.

Through Core Values and accountability structures, they figured out how to make their current situation work better. The same cramped space became more manageable when everyone had clear roles and wasn't duplicating effort. The limited budget stretched further when systematic approaches reduced waste and rework. The difficult hiring market became less critical when existing team members could handle more cases through better processes.

Rich's perspective was crucial: "We knew immediately that we could not, the two of us, the three of us, could not run the firm like we were running it." The constraint wasn't their current situation. It was their current approach to managing that situation.

Mike Griffin experienced a similar realization. Remember from Chapter 12 when he said, "I was clearly a bottleneck because I felt like I needed to be involved and have my hand in everything"? The situation wasn't the problem. The lack of systems to manage the situation was the problem.

Strategic investment thinking asks a different question: "Given our current reality, how can we work more systematically?" Instead of waiting for perfect conditions, systematic firms create better conditions through better processes.

David's firm is still in Buffalo. They're still personal injury attorneys. They still face the same market conditions. But they're growing systematically within those constraints instead of being limited by them.

Constraint 5: "The risk is too high." → "The risk of staying chaotic is higher."

This concern stops more firms than all the others combined. What if you invest time and money in systematic approaches and they don't work? What if you disrupt something that's currently functioning? What if you make things worse?

David wrestled with this exact fear. "We get comfortable. Success can be comfortable. And success can be good at one level when you're at 15 employees or 10 employees."

There's wisdom in that caution. You've built something that works, even if it's stressful. Why risk changing it?

But David came to realize that staying the same was really the highest risk of all. "Growth is not linear. It's exponential. And then it flattens out, and then it's exponential, and then it flattens out. What works for you now is not going to work for you when you have five more people reporting to you."

The risk calculation becomes clearer when you look forward instead of backward. David wasn't just protecting what he had. He was acknowledging what was coming. "We weren't at that point, but we would have had major problems within the next year or two."

> **The risk calculation becomes clearer when you look forward instead of backward.**

Rich quantified the risk of staying chaotic: "If this continues, we're going to need six more staff, including three attorneys. How are we going to train them? How are we going to manage them? We can barely manage what we have now."

The risk of implementing EOS? Time investment. Learning curve. Temporary discomfort. Possible failure.

The risk of not implementing EOS? Guaranteed chaos. Inevitable crisis. Certain burnout. Probable failure.

Chuck Welsh captured this perfectly when he finally committed after his initial skepticism. Remember his transformation from Chapter 12? "We thought we had some things figured out, but we didn't have the processes and structure we needed." They were succeeding without systems, but growth was in danger of overwhelming them.

The question isn't whether change carries risk. Of course it does. The question is whether staying chaotic carries more risk. And for every firm

I've worked with, the answer has been the same: staying chaotic is always the highest risk choice you can make.

The Investment Mindset Breakthrough

The transformation from constraint thinking to investment thinking doesn't happen overnight. But when it happens, it changes everything about how you run your firm.

David's shift is clearest in how he talks about business decisions. Before EOS, every opportunity got evaluated through scarcity: "We've never had this kind of money before. Is this going to continue? Do we really need somebody to run a marketing department?"

That's constraint thinking. Viewing every decision through what you currently lack rather than what you could build.

After EOS, David makes decisions based on what the firm needs to become. Remember his quote from earlier? "Before, I was trying to fix things that happened yesterday. Now my decisions are about fixing things six months from now."

That's investment thinking. Building capabilities that multiply over time rather than just solving immediate problems.

Rich's perspective shows the same shift. Before EOS, they reinvented responses to growth every single month. After EOS: "The profitability is going to scale along with the firm. And I feel very comfortable that we have a system in place that can grow."

Investment thinking means building once and scaling forever, rather than rebuilding monthly.

That's the mindset shift. From accepting limitations as permanent to viewing them as temporary obstacles that systematic thinking can solve.

The investment mindset shows up in three specific ways:

Time perspective shifts. Constraint thinkers ask, "Can we afford the time to implement this?" Investment thinkers ask, "Can we afford NOT to implement this, given the time it will create?"

Resource decisions change. Constraint thinkers see hiring as an expense. Investment thinkers see hiring as capacity multiplication. David went from questioning whether they needed a marketing department to systematically building capabilities that enable growth.

Risk calculation flips. Constraint thinkers see change as risky. Investment thinkers see staying chaotic as the highest risk. Rich quantified it: continuing their old approach would have created "major problems" within two years.

Investment thinking doesn't mean spending recklessly or ignoring real limitations. Chuck Welsh and his partners still work within regulatory environments, budget realities, and market conditions. But they stopped letting those constraints define what's possible and began using systematic approaches to address them.

The firms that embrace investment thinking don't just survive their constraints; they thrive. They transform them into competitive advantages.

The Cost of Constraint Thinking

I need to be careful here. Constraint thinking often comes from a responsible place. You're being thoughtful with time, money, and energy that feel limited. That's not wrong.

But there's an opportunity cost worth considering.

While you're carefully evaluating whether you can afford to implement systems, other firms with nearly identical constraints are building systematic capabilities. While you're waiting for better conditions, systematic firms are creating better conditions through better processes.

The gap grows over time. Think back to David's schedule and the 16 people interrupting him daily, that will soon be 4. That's 5–12 hours of strategic time per week, every week, for years. Over three years, that's hundreds of hours of high-value work focused on growth instead of fire-fighting.

While constraint-focused firms are still solving the same problems month after month, systematic firms are building momentum.

That competitive advantage grows exponentially. Systematic firms don't just solve their current constraints; they also address future ones. They build capabilities that enable them to handle larger constraints. David's firm can now absorb growth that would have overwhelmed their previous approach. They've created systematic capacity for problems they haven't even encountered yet.

Think about what systematic firms achieve while others hesitate:

Time constraints become systematic efficiency. Regulatory complexity becomes compliance confidence. Small size becomes an agility advantage. Current limitations become strategic opportunities.

The choice isn't whether you have constraints. Every firm has constraints. The choice is whether you'll focus on your limitations or your opportunities.

The choice is whether you'll focus on your limitations or your opportunities.

David, Rich, Mike, and Chuck all had the same constraints you do. Tight budgets. Limited time. Regulatory complexity. Difficult hiring markets. They chose to work systematically within those constraints rather than letting them define what's possible.

That choice made all the difference.

You've seen the evidence. David and Rich transformed their Buffalo personal injury practice from monthly crisis mode to systematic growth. Mike and Chuck went from operating silos to coordinated teams running two businesses. They didn't do it by eliminating their constraints. They did it by working systematically within them.

The choice isn't whether you have constraints. The choice is whether you'll focus on your limitations or your opportunities.

The choice is whether you'll focus on your limitations or your opportunities.

But here's where the conversation takes an interesting turn.

Once you embrace systematic thinking and start seeing results, you'll face a challenge you'll want to have. It's what happens when EOS works so well that you outgrow the basics and need to scale beyond initial implementation.

Remember Rich Hall's projection? "Three years from now, we'll probably be doubled in size. The profitability is going to scale along with the firm."

That's not just growth. That's exponential scaling enabled by systematic thinking.

Success creates sophisticated opportunities that require advanced approaches. When your firm doubles, triples, or explodes past your original vision, you need systems that can handle that complexity.

In the next chapter, let me show you what that success problem looks like and how to solve it.

Chapter Fourteen

Scaling Beyond EOS Basics: A Good Problem to Have

You've overcome the constraints and embraced systematic thinking. You've seen how Mike, Chuck, David, and Rich transformed their firms through disciplined execution. Now let me tell you about a problem you're going to want to have.

It's what happens when EOS works so well that you outgrow the basics and need to scale beyond initial implementation.

The Success Problem

Four and a half years into his EOS journey, Lin McCraw had achieved what most firm owners only dream about and then discovered he could dream exponentially bigger.

Here's some more detail about his firm. His personal injury practice exploded from the $2.5 million range to $14–15 million in revenue, with a clear path to $30 million by 2030. He went from being a capable operator trying to run everything himself to becoming a true CEO with the confidence to scale across multiple markets and locations.

"I was a good operator, could handle a great lawsuit, could get stuff done," Lin explained. "But this has allowed me to grow into a better CEO. It's allowed me the room to think outside the everyday, to think about what my employees need, to think about where I think the market is going, what I think we really need, and position the firm to get there."

Lin discovered that mastering EOS had created opportunities he'd never imagined possible, something most firm owners never get to experience. His confidence had transformed from managing a single location to knowing he could systematically scale to massive proportions.

"I never dreamed of having more than one location. I could have 50 of them, and I can make them run now. I know I can."

Think about that for a second. From never dreaming of a second location to confidently projecting 50. That's not delusion. That's what systematic thinking does when it compounds over time.

This is the success problem. When basic EOS tools work so magnificently that your firm grows beyond what those tools were initially implemented to handle, it's not a failure of the system. It's evidence that the system worked exactly as intended. Now you get to apply systematic thinking to increasingly sophisticated opportunities that create generational wealth and impact.

Lin's journey illustrates the five most exciting scaling opportunities that successful EOS firms get to pursue. If you're implementing EOS now, understanding these opportunities helps you prepare for the extraordinary possibilities that systematic growth creates. And if you're already scaling, you'll recognize exactly where you are in this progression.

Opportunity 1: Leadership Leverage (From Owner-Dependent to Visionary-Driven)

Lin's first scaling opportunity was evolving from operator to true CEO while building leadership depth that could multiply his impact across multiple locations and markets. When he started EOS, Lin was the classic capable operator trying to run everything himself.

The transformation wasn't just about delegation. It was about developing the confidence and systems to scale leadership across multiple organizations.

The transformation wasn't just about delegation. It was about developing the confidence and systems to scale leadership across multiple operations. EOS gave Lin the foundation, but scaling beyond $15 million requires more sophisticated leadership development and delegation frameworks.

"EOS gave me confidence that I could grow it. And when I saw it actually happening, it gave me confidence to make those decisions faster and to take bigger risks because I knew I really wasn't taking a huge risk because now I've got a reliable operating system in place."

Lynn St. Louis of the Elder Law Group of Washington experienced a similar leadership evolution, though on a different scale. Bringing in Randie, an experienced Integrator, didn't just solve current problems; it also set the stage for future success. It gave Lynn the capacity to develop other leaders and pursue opportunities she never had time for before. "The single biggest change that EOS created in my firm? It was the Integrator. It was a people thing."

Leadership leverage opportunity means systematically developing people who can develop others, creating exponential growth in your firm's capabilities across multiple locations and markets. You need leaders who can create more leaders. You need enough leadership capacity that your Visionary truly has time to be visionary about opportunities that can transform entire markets.

Opportunity 2: Geographic and Market Expansion

Lin's second scaling opportunity involved the thrilling realization that systematic thinking creates the confidence to scale across multiple locations and markets. When you master EOS basics, geographic expansion becomes an exciting strategic opportunity rather than an overwhelming challenge.

In the past, he wondered, "How do you manage somebody from that far away? How do you make sure they're doing what they're supposed to? We've got that figured out now."

Lin's confidence shift is the kind of transformation that creates massive wealth. He went from thinking small and local to understanding that systematic operations can scale across unlimited geographic markets. The systems he'd mastered for one location became the blueprint for exponential expansion.

"Once you have a little bit of experience with it, once you see it run, then you realize, oh, this isn't rocket science. It's just plug and play."

Lynn St. Louis experienced similar expansion opportunities, though hers focused more on service line development and market sophistication. Her firm evolved from basic estate planning to a comprehensive, sophisticated practice capable of serving its clients throughout their lifetimes and as their needs evolved.

The geographic and market expansion opportunity means confidently deciding which markets to enter, timing expansion investments for maximum impact, and building capabilities that can support multiple locations or practice areas simultaneously. This is where systematic thinking creates exponential wealth rather than just linear improvements.

Opportunity 3:
Financial Sophistication and Growth Capital

Lin's third scaling opportunity was the exciting reality that massive growth requires strategic investment, and systematic firms can confidently make those investments at unprecedented scales. His firm's path from $2.5 million to $14–15 million, targeting $30 million by 2030, required sophisticated financial planning and capital allocation.

In talking about his 10-Year Target of $30M by '30, Lin said, "We made some really cool hires. I think we'll get there early. I think we'll get there by probably '27 or '28."

This level of confident, ambitious financial planning is only possible when you have systematic operations that support strategic investment decisions. Lin isn't hoping to hit $30 million. He's systematically building toward it and expects to arrive early.

Lynn St. Louis experienced the same financial sophistication challenges. As her revenues climb toward $5 million, her profits are temporarily down as she invests in capabilities that will support even bigger growth. Growth is always a cash monster, but it's a beautiful monster when you're feeding it systematically.

The financial sophistication opportunity includes making strategic decisions about massive growth investments, evaluating expansion opportunities worth millions, and having financial leadership that can guide decisions at scales most firms never reach. Many firms at this stage get to work with fractional CFO expertise that makes the difference between crippling growth and wealth-creating growth.

Opportunity 4:
Advanced Systems and Technology Integration

Lin's fourth scaling opportunity involved building sophisticated systems that could coordinate multiple locations, advanced metrics, and technology platforms into a competitive advantage that smaller firms couldn't match. When you scale EOS, you need systems that can handle complexity while maintaining simplicity.

"Once you start getting a little higher up, you're in a position where we've got to do things like get one number for each person, and we've got to elevate that in The Accountability Chart."

Lin recognized that scaling to $30 million across multiple locations required more sophisticated accountability systems, advanced Scorecarding, and technology integration beyond what his initial EOS Scorecard provided. But because he'd mastered the fundamentals, building advanced systems became an exciting challenge rather than an overwhelming obstacle.

Lynn St. Louis experienced similar opportunities for technology integration. She is coordinating multiple experts for financial dashboards, tech stack optimization, and other specialists for marketing and process development. "I want everything structured. I want processes, and I want them searchable."

The advanced systems opportunity means connecting sophisticated technology platforms, implementing advanced metrics and accountability systems, and creating operational superiority that generates sustainable competitive advantages. This is where systematic thinking creates capabilities that transform entire markets.

Opportunity 5: Strategic Vision and Market Leadership

Lin's fifth scaling opportunity involved the thrilling realization that systematic operations create the foundation for true market leadership and strategic vision that can reshape entire industries. Advanced EOS implementation creates the confidence and capacity for strategic thinking at unprecedented levels.

Lin's transformation from operator to strategic market thinker exemplifies what becomes possible when systematic operations free visionaries to truly be visionary. He's not just running a bigger firm. He's positioning his firm to lead market transformation.

"By having that vision, it gives everybody a goal they can align toward, values where they know that decisions are going to be made through those filters."

Lynn St. Louis recognized similar strategic opportunities. Her firm had built assets and capabilities that could support sophisticated market development, though she admitted, "I've got a great YouTube channel. It's got over 10,000 followers, but we're not doing shit with it." The opportunities were there. She just needed the strategic frameworks to systematically capitalize on them.

The strategic vision opportunity includes confidently pursuing market leadership positions, building capabilities that reshape industry standards, and creating wealth through systematic competitive advantages that establish true market dominance.

Advanced Architecture Using EOS Tools

Pursuing these scaling opportunities required Lin to move beyond basic tools to more sophisticated applications of systematic thinking.

Advanced Leadership Development meant multi-level leadership training across multiple locations, succession planning, and approaches to developing decision-making capabilities that multiply impact exponentially.

Sophisticated Market Expansion Systems included geographic expansion frameworks, multi-location management systems, and approaches to market entry that enable confident scaling.

Financial Intelligence Platforms covered advanced dashboard development, unit economics tracking across multiple locations, growth-investment analysis, and strategic financial planning capabilities that enable confident decision-making at massive scales.

Process Architecture involved workflow design across multiple locations, technology platform integration, quality assurance frameworks, and continuous improvement methodologies that create sustainable competitive advantages.

Strategic Market Leadership Capabilities meant market analysis frameworks, competitive positioning strategies, expansion planning methodologies, and approaches to industry transformation that generate generational wealth.

"It's like an operating system for your computer. I know when I fire it up what's going to come on and where my emails are. I know where my stuff is. That is what EOS does for you. It allows you to look up and look out."

It's not that he has outgrown EOS; it's that he is using more sophisticated tools built on the deceptively simple EOS framework.

Looking Forward

If you're just starting your EOS journey, Lin's scaling opportunities might seem like distant possibilities. But understanding what extraordinary success looks like helps you build foundations that can support explosive growth when you're ready.

The firms that scale successfully aren't the ones that abandon systematic thinking when they encounter sophisticated opportunities. They're the ones who apply systematic thinking to increasingly complex situations.

"Once you see it running and see it successful, it becomes a proven concept. And with your team members, a lot of them have to see it, especially with lawyers, because lawyers are very smart rats."

Lin's insight captures the essence of scaling beyond basics. The fundamental principles remain the same, but their application becomes more sophisticated, and the returns become exponential as your firm grows toward market leadership.

Your firm has potential you haven't even begun to tap. But success at scale requires more than good intentions. It requires systematic foundations that can support extraordinary growth.

Ready to build something bigger than yourself?

Chapter Fifteen

What Really Matters: Getting Your Life Back

We've talked about systems and growth, revenue targets, and operational efficiency. We've explored the mechanics of building a firm that runs without you. But let's pause for a moment and remember what this is really about.

It's not about creating the perfect accountability chart or mastering quarterly planning sessions, though those matter. It's not about optimizing profit margins or scaling to multiple locations, though those create options.

This is about getting your life back. This is about building something extraordinary while finally having the freedom to fully live the life you've been working toward all along.

The Life You Actually Get to Live

Remember Constance? The immigration attorney from Chapter 1 who was drowning in operational chaos, working weekends, and wondering if she'd ever be able to step away from the daily grind without everything falling apart?

Here's what Tuesday morning looks like for her now.

She's working from her home office in Texas. Not because there's an emergency. Not because she's putting out fires. Because she chooses to. Her immigration firm spans multiple states with offices in Houston, Atlanta,

Phoenix, Vegas, and a new acquisition in Denver, but she doesn't have to be physically present for any of it to run smoothly.

"My office is like two miles away," Constance tells me. "Unless I have an in-person meeting, I don't really go. When I'm in town, I'll make an appearance, but I might stay a few hours for whatever in-person things I have and come back home."

Think about that for a second. The owner of a 450-person, multi-million-dollar law firm who doesn't have to live at the office. Who can work from home or from anywhere because her systems work effectively. Who can trust her team to run the business because she's built a business with systems that give them freedom and keep them within the lines.

This isn't some fantasy scenario I'm painting for motivation. This is Constance's reality. The same woman who three years earlier was the chief fire extinguisher in a firm that seemed designed to spontaneously combust.

What Weekends Look Like Now

"And then, of course, now I have a boyfriend, which I didn't have before. And I like to spend time with him. So I actually hike on weekends. We're hanging out and having fun and doing stuff."

Read that again. Constance is dating. She has weekends. She has a personal life that doesn't get consumed by work emergencies because she's built systems that prevent most emergencies from happening in the first place.

This isn't about work-life balance, that tired concept that assumes work and life are in constant tension. This is about work-life integration, where your business amplifies your personal life rather than destroying it.

When you build something systematic and valuable, you create the freedom to truly enjoy the relationships and experiences that matter most.

It is about work-life integration, where your business amplifies your personal life rather than destroying it.

This year is her son's senior year of high school, and for the first time in her career, Constance doesn't have to choose between being present for his milestones and keeping her firm running. She can attend college visits without checking emails every ten minutes. She can be fully present at his final football games, graduation planning meetings, and all those once-in-a-lifetime moments that working parents often miss because of office commitments.

Senior year happens once. Graduation happens once. Those conversations about your child's future happen once. Constance gets to experience all of it because she built a business that amplifies her life rather than consuming it.

Travel That's Actually About Living

"I'm still traveling quite a bit. So there's that. I got a fractional ownership with NetJets, which has helped a lot. Because now I can do a day trip. I can fly up to Denver and back in a day, Vegas and back in a day, stuff that I couldn't do before."

Constance travels extensively, sometimes three times a week. But here's the thing. She's not putting out fires or chasing problems. She's building strategic relationships, exploring new markets, and living the kind of life that financial freedom and operational excellence make possible.

She drives through Colorado to run trail races, not checking emails every five minutes but entirely present and engaged. She notices the small towns, the opportunities, the communities that need her services. Not as a stressed-out attorney looking for the next emergency, but as a strategic visionary seeing possibilities.

"I was going to stay in Aspen, and I realized, somebody has got to make the bed. Somebody has got to wash the dishes. Someone's got to chop the vegetables. And most likely, they all need to become citizens."

She sees the immigrant communities, the service workers, the people who need advocates. And she has the systematic capacity to serve them at scale. That's what happens when you build a business instead of just practicing law.

Building Generational Impact

"We just started a nonprofit. We're working on our Mexican entity. So I'm able to have all these ideas and things that I want to do and bring them to the table."

Constance isn't just building wealth. She's building generational impact through the Wannamaker Foundation and what she calls "Wannamaker University." Her vision extends far beyond legal services to community centers in multiple offices, English classes, citizenship classes, and financial literacy programs.

"My vision is to have all these different offices be little community centers. We're doing a lot of Know Your Rights stuff these days in our different offices. And now we're going to start doing them virtually as well."

This is the kind of visionary thinking that becomes possible when you're not spending your days putting out fires. When your firm runs like a well-oiled machine, you have the mental bandwidth and financial resources to think about legacy, impact, and the kind of change you want to create in the world.

"I really feel strongly that we need to create more citizens. Often, one of the biggest barriers for people who are residents to become an actual citizen is that they can't learn English. So we're going to help with that."

Constance is building educational programs, partnering with community colleges, and creating sliding-scale services that serve her community while driving business growth. She's not choosing between profit and purpose. Systematic thinking has given her the foundation to pursue both simultaneously.

Strategic Growth from Strength

"We're talking about having personal injury as a service. Probably in Q1 of next year, we'll start working on that. And just because of the political environment, I am not necessarily putting out fires, but I have to stay on top of all this shit that's happening in the world."

Even in challenging political environments, Constance isn't reactive. She's strategic. She's expanding into personal injury, building a Mexican entity, and acquiring firms in multiple markets. But she's doing it from a position of strength, with systems that can handle complexity and a team that can execute her vision.

"Now we have hired a VP of strategic initiatives. She's on our leadership team. So all these projects, like the nonprofit that nobody else has the bandwidth to really get going, she can work on. And at the Wannamaker University, she'll be working with a consultant to get that done."

This is what sophisticated leadership looks like. Constance doesn't have to do everything herself. She's built a team with the bandwidth and expertise to execute multiple strategic initiatives simultaneously. She can pursue generational wealth building and community impact because her operational foundation supports both.

The Unicorn: When Entrepreneurship Meets Mission

Here's what makes Constance extraordinary. She's that rare lawyer who embodies both the entrepreneurial drive and the cause-based mission. Most attorneys fall clearly into one camp or the other. Either they're building businesses for growth and wealth, or they're fighting for justice and social change.

Constance is the unicorn who proves you don't have to choose.

Her entrepreneurial side drives the multi-state expansion, the strategic acquisitions, and the wealth-building activities. Her cause-based side drives the Wannamaker Foundation, the community centers, the English and citizenship classes, and the commitment to serving immigrant communities who desperately need advocates.

The key insight? EOS didn't force her to choose between profit and purpose. It gave her the operational foundation to pursue both at unprecedented scales. She can build generational wealth while creating generational impact because systematic thinking paired with a solid operating system multiplies everything, including your capacity for meaning.

EOS didn't force a choice between profit and purpose.

For entrepreneurial lawyers, Constance proves that systematic thinking can create the kind of wealth and freedom most attorneys only dream about. For cause-based lawyers, she demonstrates that building a sophisticated business amplifies your mission rather than compromising it.

Most attorneys think they have to choose between building wealth and building impact. Constance chose EOS and got both.

What This Means for You

If you're reading this thinking, "That sounds amazing, but my firm is nowhere near that level," you're missing the point.

Constance didn't start with a 450-person firm and NetJets access. She started with chaos, stress, and the same overwhelming challenges you're probably facing right now.

"I think I felt like I was putting out a lot of fires, always dealing with messes," she remembered about the old days. Sound familiar?

The transformation happened because she implemented EOS to build something bigger than herself. She created systems that could run without her, teams that could make decisions independently, and processes that could handle complexity while maintaining quality.

The life you want isn't waiting for you to reach some arbitrary revenue number or firm size. It's waiting for you to build systems that create freedom. It's waiting for you to think like a business owner, not just a lawyer. It's waiting for you to apply the same systematic approach you use in legal work to building an organization that serves your life rather than consuming it.

Your EOS Future

Picture yourself two years from now. You're not chained to your desk, not putting out fires every day, not missing important personal moments because of work. Your firm runs smoothly whether you're in the office or not. Your team makes good decisions independently because they have clear systems and accountability structures in place.

You have the financial freedom to make strategic investments, the time freedom to pursue relationships and experiences that matter, and the operational freedom to focus on the highest-value work that only you can do.

Maybe you're building a foundation like Constance, or expanding into multiple markets, or simply having dinner with your family without checking your phone every five minutes. Maybe you're dating again, or taking real vacations, or pursuing hobbies you abandoned years ago when the firm consumed your life.

This isn't fantasy. This is what EOS creates for lawyers who choose to build businesses rather than just practice law.

The choice is yours. You can keep managing chaos, hoping things will somehow get better on their own. Or you can start building the systems that create the life you want to live.

Constance chose systems. She chose to think bigger. She chose to build something extraordinary that serves her life rather than dominating it.

What will you choose?

In our final chapter, we'll explore exactly how to get started on this transformation because understanding what's possible is just the beginning. The real

You can start building the systems that create the life you want to live.

question is what you're going to do about it. How do you take the first step toward the life and business you actually want to build?

That's where we're going next. Because the best time to start building a system was five years ago. The second-best time is right now.

Chapter Sixteen

How to Get Started: Your Next Step Forward

You've seen what's possible. You've witnessed Lynn's transformation from constraint thinking to methodical growth. You've watched Lin build a firm that's scaling from $15 million toward $30 million with confidence. You've experienced Constance's journey to complete life freedom while building generational wealth and impact.

The transformation happened because they applied EOS to their firm to build something bigger than themselves.

Now the question is: how do you make this real for you?

The Implementation Reality

Let me be honest about something. There's a gap between knowing and doing that trips up most attorneys. You can read every business book ever written, attend every conference, and understand every framework, but none of that matters if you don't actually implement change in your firm.

I've seen brilliant lawyers who could explain EOS concepts perfectly but couldn't make them stick in their organizations. I've watched firms start strong with quarterly planning sessions and weekly meetings, only to gradually slide back into chaos because they lacked the discipline or guidance to maintain momentum.

The choice you're facing isn't really about whether EOS works. You've seen the evidence. The choice is about how you'll implement it and what support you need to make it successful.

Two Paths Forward

Based on my experience, there are two viable approaches to EOS implementation: self-implementation and professional guidance. Both can work, but they work differently and require different commitments.

The Self-Implementation Path

Some attorneys successfully implement EOS on their own. Rich, David, and Marc Schneider all started this way. I did it myself when we had four people at my CFO company, and it went beautifully.

Self-implementation makes sense when you have a smaller firm (typically under 10 people), a limited budget for professional services, and high personal discipline for maintaining systems over time. You'll need someone on your team who can facilitate meetings effectively and hold people accountable to the process.

The advantages are obvious. Lower cost, complete control over the pace and approach, and the satisfaction of building something yourself. Many of the tools and resources are readily available through books, online materials, Scalinglaw.com, and the EOS community resources.

But let me tell you what happened to me. We eventually got lazy and had to re-implement EOS. And the second time we tried self-implementation, it didn't go as well as the first. We got sloppy. Meetings didn't always follow the L10 agenda. We didn't dig deep enough to find the root causes of the issues. We didn't really put the important issues on the issues list; we just put the easy ones we could knock off quickly. Rocks weren't getting done. Our Scorecard was all red, and nobody was doing anything about it.

Sound familiar? Success with self-implementation requires ongoing discipline that's harder to maintain than most people realize.

The Professional Guidance Path

After our second failed attempt at self-implementation, I emailed Gino Wickman directly. He'd written quotes for the front of a couple of my books, so I figured I had some credibility. I wrote this email that, if print-ed, would have been 15 pages long, explaining everything that was going wrong.

Gino wrote back: "Brooke, it would take me all day just to figure out what's in this email. Answer these five questions, and I'll give you a good Implementer."

That implementer changed my life. But more than that, working with our Implementer taught me something I couldn't learn through self-im-plementation. The biggest breakthrough centered on trust. We had not built trust within our leadership team, and that lack of trust filtered down throughout the entire firm.

An Implementer sees what you can't see. They facilitate the uncomfort-able conversations. They hold you accountable for the decisions you keep postponing. They help you move faster because they've done this hundreds of times and know what works.

Professional implementation makes sense when you have 10 or more people or complex operations, when speed of implementation matters, when you need external accountability to maintain momentum, and when your time is better spent on strategic work than learning facilitation.

What Makes an Excellent EOS Implementer

Not all EOS Implementers are created equal, and not all of them under-stand law firms. Here's what to look for.

EOS Worldwide Training

Anybody can read *Traction* and try to hang out a shingle. There are hun-dreds of people doing it. The problem is that without the formal EOS training, they only know part of the story. They are not dedicated to continually learning and honing their skills in a community of people who share knowledge. Chuck and Mike of ACCEL Law Group started out this way and regret the wasted months with a group that had nothing but the best of intentions.

Deep EOS Experience

You want someone who lives and breathes the methodology. They should have worked with dozens of companies and seen what works and what doesn't. They should know the tools cold and understand how they interconnect.

Law Firm Specialization

This matters more than you might think. Law firms have unique dynamics. Partner relationships, billable-hour pressures, trust accounting requirements, ethical obligations, and the attorney's personality all create challenges that generic business consultants don't understand.

An implementer who specializes in law firms will recognize patterns immediately. They'll know why your partners resist giving up control, why your team struggles with delegation, and why lawyers want to debate every process instead of just trying it. They will also understand that the way you build your Accountability Chart on your first day together is going to affect the compensation structure you roll out at the beginning of the year.

Financial Integration

The best EOS Implementers understand that you can't separate operational systems from financial systems. They should be able to connect your EOS Scorecard to your financial metrics, help you build Rocks that drive profitability, and ensure your vision aligns with your financial reality.

Proven Results

Ask for references from firms similar to yours. Not just testimonials, but actual conversations with other law firm owners who have worked with this person. What results did they see? How long did it take? What surprised them about the process?

Red Flags to Avoid

Watch out for generic business consultants without EOS expertise who think they can read the books and help you implement EOS. Or just apply general principles to your firm. Avoid EOS Implementers without law firm experience who don't understand your unique challenges. Run from anyone promising unrealistic timelines or results. And be wary of anyone who lacks a clear process or methodology.

Smart Questions to Ask

When you're interviewing potential Implementers, here are the questions that will reveal whether they're a good fit for you.

About Their Experience

How many law firms have you worked with using EOS? What specific challenges do law firms face with EOS implementation that other businesses don't? Can you provide references from firms similar in size and practice area to mine?

About Results

What measurable results should we expect and when? How do you track progress and ensure accountability? What happens if we're not achieving expected outcomes?

The Investment Framework

Let's talk about cost, because I know that's on your mind. Professional EOS implementation isn't cheap, but it's also not the most expensive mistake you can make. The most expensive mistake is continuing to run your firm chaotically, missing growth opportunities, and burning yourself out in the process.

Think about it this way. What's the cost of not implementing systematic operations? What's the value of your time that you're currently spending on operational firefighting? What growth opportunities are you missing because you can't scale beyond your personal capacity?

Most firms see measurable improvements within the first quarter and full ROI within the first year. However, the real value isn't just financial. It's the freedom to work on your business instead of being trapped in it.

But here's the real deal: EOS comes with a guarantee. First of all, there are no contracts; you hire your Implementer for the day. If it goes well, you can hire them for another one. If not, you never have to see them again. But even better, you don't pay until the day is over, and you decide whether you got value.

Talk about lowering the risk!

Getting Started Today

Self-implementation vs. an EOS Implementer, regardless of which path you choose, here's how to start building momentum immediately.

First, read Gino Wickman's *Traction*. Though if you'd rather read more of a story, less of a textbook, you might enjoy Gino Wickman and Mike Paton's *Get A Grip* more. Same material, different presentation. Get a foundational understanding of EOS principles. Even if you hire an Implementer, you'll get better results if you understand the system.

Second, assess your current state. Honestly evaluate where your firm stands today. What's working? What's broken? Where are the biggest pain points? To help you do this, you can take an Organizational Checkup free of charge at

Third, identify your leadership team. Who would sit in the room with you? Who has the capability and commitment to drive organizational change?

Fourth, start with one tool. Pick one EOS tool and implement it consistently. Many firms start with weekly Level 10 Meetings because they create immediate visibility into issues and accountability.

The Most Important Decision

Here's what I want you to understand. The choice between self-implementation and professional guidance isn't the most important decision you'll make. The most important decision is whether you'll implement EOS or continue managing chaos.

> **The most important decision is whether you'll implement EOS or continue managing chaos.**

Every day you wait is another day of missed opportunities, unnecessary stress, and limited growth. Every week you spend firefighting problems instead of building systems is a week you can't get back.

Lin McCraw understood this when he fully committed to the EOS implementation. "It elevates you as a business owner," he explained.

The systematic thinking that creates these results is available to you right now. The tools exist. The framework has been proven. The only question is whether you'll start using it.

What You're Going to Build

The firm you want to build, the life you want to live, the impact you want to create. All of it starts with EOS. All of it becomes possible when you stop managing chaos and start building something intentional.

What you've seen in this book isn't luck or natural talent. It's the result of systematic thinking applied consistently over time within a proven framework. The same systematic thinking you use to win cases, serve clients, and build legal strategies.

You already have the skills you need. You just need to start applying them to building the business that will give you the life you truly want to live.

The choice is yours. What are you going to build?

Acknowledgments

Every time I write a book, I thank all the clients, current and former, who taught me so much over the years and allow me to share their stories.

This time it's different. This time, clients agreed to let me use their names, their firms' names, revenue numbers, internal goals, and incredibly personal stories. This time, they put their names and reputations on the line just as much as I have to help you understand the incredible value of EOS. And for that, I want to thank each of them individually.

Mike Griffin - ACCEL Law Group

Rich Hall - Cantor, Wolff, Nicastro and Hall, LLC

Lin McCraw - McCraw Law Group

J. P. Pendergast - Pendergast Law

Moumita Rahman - The Law Firm of Moumita Rahman, PLLC

Marc Schneider - Schneider Buchel LLP

Mike Smith - Smith Barid, LLC

Lynn St Louis - ELG Estate Planning

Constance Wannamaker - C. R. Wannamaker Law, PLLC

David Wolff - Cantor, Wolff, Nicastro and Hall, LLC

Chuck Welsh - ACCEL Law Group

I never would have been able to complete this book without them.

About the Author

Brooke Lively helps law firm leaders stop running on chaos and finally get what they want from their businesses: clarity, traction, and healthy, profitable growth. A serial entrepreneur who has assisted hundreds of law firms over the last 20 years, she blends sharp financial expertise (MBA, CFA) with a smart, direct, and refreshingly human approach that cuts through the b.s. and makes scaling a law firm feel less painful...and a lot more intentional.

Brooke is an international bestselling author and industry thought leader. Scaling Law is her seventh book and the first and only EOS Worldwide–published book exclusively for lawyers. Scaling Law discusses how to implement EOS in a way that actually works inside the uniquely complex business of law.

Connect with Brooke at ScalingLaw.com when you're ready to stop running your law firm on adrenaline and start running it like a real business.

EOS®
IMPACT
The exclusive publishing
imprint for EOS
Implementers through
a collaboration with
Igniting Souls.
IgnitingSouls.com/EOSImpact

The EOS® Platform People Love

Mange EOS®, projects, people, performance, process, and surveys - all in one platform.

RUNNING YOUR FIRM ON EOS?

DO IT WITH A
COMMUNITY OF SUPPORT

Scaling Law helps law firms implement EOS without the chaos, fluff or trial and error.

HOW?

Community

Connect with other lawyers who are implementing EOS that get the challenges and realities of running a law firm.

Resources

Get practical articles and short videos with real-world best practices to help you apply EOS in real time with less talk and more action.

Implementers

Find EOS Implementers who are trained, experienced, and fluent in law firm dynamics-matched to your firm's size, goals, and leadership style.

EOS Works.
The Right Support Makes It Last.

Discover Actionable Advice to Eliminate Financial Stress and Increase Your Bottom Line.

BrookeLively.com

Running A Law Firm Is Hard. Running One Well Takes FINANCIAL LEADERSHIP

Cathcap provides fractional CFO Services exclusively for law firms. Allowing you to build stronger, better-run firms that create clarity, control, and options.